ETHICS AND THE MARKET

Ethics and the Market

Edited by
RICHARD NORMAN
University of Kent

Ashgate

Aldershot • Brookfield USA • Singapore • Sydney

Published by
Ashgate Publishing Ltd
Gower House
Croft Road
Aldershot
Hants GU11 3HR
England

Ashgate Publishing Company
Old Post Road
Brookfield
Vermont 05036
USA

British Library Cataloguing in Publication Data
Norman, Richard
    Ethics and the market
    1. Business ethics
    I. Title II. Society for Applied Philosophy
    174.4

Library of Congress Catalog Card Number: 99-72337

ISBN 1 84014 980 9

Printed and bound by Athenaeum Press, Ltd.,
Gateshead, Tyne & Wear.

Contents

v

List of Contributors

Richard Norman is Chair of the Society for Applied Philosophy, and Professor of Moral Philosophy at the University of Kent. His publications include *The Moral Philosophers* (2nd edn. 1998) and *Ethics, Killing and War* (1995).

Raymond Plant was Senior Lecturer in Philosophy at Manchester University until 1979 when he became Professor of Politics at Southampton University. He is now Master of St. Catherine's College, Oxford. He has published *Political Philosophy and Social Welfare*; *Hegel*; *Philosophy, Politics and Citizenship*; *Hegel on Religion*; and *Modern Political Thought*.

Patrick Shaw is a senior lecturer in Philosophy at Glasgow University. His publications include *Logic and its Limits* (2nd edn. 1997).

Theo van Willigenburg is professor of Moral Philosophy in the Faculty of Philosophy, Erasmus University Rotterdam. He works in the field of applied ethics (medical ethics / business ethics) and ethical theory (meta-ethics).

J.E.J. Altham is Sidgwick Lecturer in Philosophy in the University of Cambridge, and a Fellow of Gonville and Caius College.

Toby Lowe is about to complete a PhD in Political Philosophy at the University of Newcastle upon Tyne. He is attempting to produce a positive communitarian framework which locates the traditional communitarian ethical concerns within a model that recognises the influence of political, economic and social power.

Barbara Goodwin is Professor of Politics at the University of East Anglia, Norwich. Her recent publications include *Justice by Lottery* and the fourth edition of *Using Political Ideas*.

Phillip Cole is Principal Lecturer in Applied Philosophy at Middlesex University. His publications include *The Free, the Unfree and the Excluded; a Treatise on the Conditions of Liberty* (Ashgate 1998). He is currently writing a book on political philosophy and immigration.

David Merrill lectures on the history of political philosophy and modern ideologies at the University of Reading. He previously completed a doctorate in political theory at the University of Southampton.

C.R.E.H. Descombes is currently completing research with the Open University. Her previous research projects have included the nature of the doctor-patient relationship and ethical issues in health care rationing.

Terry Newholm is researching Ethical Consumers at the Open University Centre for Complexity and Change, and lecturing part-time in political theory at DeMontfort University.

Preface

Many thanks to the contributors whose papers are collected in this volume, for delivering their copy so promptly and cooperating so helpfully at every stage, and to the Ashgate editorial staff for their valuable advice and guidance. Special thanks are due to Elizabeth Shihabi, who has performed heroic feats of combat with wordprocessing programmes and recalcitrant formats in order to produce copy for publication.

The papers in the collection originated as contributions to the 1998 Annual Conference of the Society for Applied Philosophy. The topic for the conference was proposed by Professor Alan Milne, who then selected the papers and drew up the programme. We were very disappointed to learn, just a few days before the conference, that he would be prevented by illness from attending, and our disappointment turned to shocked grief when we learned of his death a week later. He had been one of the most regular and dedicated contributors to previous conferences, and his commitment to philosophical enquiry and its application to the world of public affairs was an inspiration to us all. This volume is, with gratitude and affection, dedicated to his memory.

Introduction

RICHARD NORMAN

The chapters in this book do not presuppose or defend any general ideological stance on the ethics of markets. They do not share the naive assumption of free-market libertarians that the untramelled functioning of market institutions will, just by itself, ensure morally acceptable outcomes. They recognise nevertheless that market economies are with us for the foreseeable future and that we had better address the ethical questions which they pose. They vary in their assessment of the ethical acceptability of market relations. Some of the papers present thorough-going moral critiques of markets. Others maintain than in some areas market relationships may be able to survive moral criticism more successfully than the alternatives. But all the chapters start from the acknowledgement that the ethical acceptability of markets is at least an open question.

The book has been divided into two parts. The chapters in Part I address at a relatively general level the relation between markets and fundamental values. Those in Part II consider the relations between market institutions and other social institutions and practices, discussing the moral ethos of privatised industries and services in comparison with the public sector, the relevance of market institutions to questions of poverty and social justice, the role of market relations in the health service, and the idea of the 'ethical consumer'. The division between the two Parts is not a sharp one, it is merely a difference in degrees of generality and specificity. The chapters in Part II continue many of the themes of Part I, but do so with more reference to the empirical features of particular social institutions.

The opening chapter, by Raymond Plant, sets out a broad map of the terrain in which many of the subsequent papers will be located. Distinguishing between a 'market economy' and a 'market society', Plant identifies the moral limits which need to be set to market values and motivations in order to prevent them from dominating the rest of society. He explores three ways in which markets require moral boundaries to be set. First, though markets depend on the operation of self-interest, they are *underpinned* by values, such as civic virtues, which cannot themselves be

1

derived purely from self-interest. Secondly, limits need to be set to the *scope* of the market. Certain kinds of goods and services may be distorted if they are treated simply as things to be bought or sold, and Plant discusses cases such as the sale of human organs, the importance of the service ethic in the public sector, and the dangers of the commodification of values such as those of sexual and family relationships. Thirdly, markets have *outcomes* which are subject to criticism from the standpoint of social justice, and Plant notes in particular that the claimed 'trickle-down' effect cannot be invoked to defend the inequalities of power which are created by markets.

The moral problems which are most deeply built into the operations of markets are those raised by the motivations of market entrepreneurs, and those raised by the evaluations of market consumers. Patrick Shaw picks up the issue of the conflict between moral values and the self-interested motivation of market transactions, and suggests that markets foster a kind of moral minimalism in the sense that 'moral standards are set by the behaviour of the worst'. Competition drives down moral standards because those who are bound by scruples lose out to those whose pursuit of self-interest is unfettered by such scruples. Though this is an inherent tendency of markets, it is not an inevitable feature of market societies, since the regulation of markets is possible, most obviously by the state, but Shaw is not sanguine about the possibility of morally effective regulation in practice.

Theo van Willigenburg focuses on the standpoint of the consumer, and on the reduction of value to the satisfaction of preferences, as expressed by the price which goods which will fetch in the market. He warns against over-hasty and over-simple arguments criticising such a reduction, arguments which he refers to as the 'argument from objectivity' and the 'argument from intrinsic value'. He nevertheless concludes that not all value can be reduced to market value. The consumer is not always right.

The distinction between the satisfaction of preferences and the quality of life is important for the argument of J. E. J. Altham's chapter. He invokes a concept of efficiency which he takes from the work of Schumacher, which contrasts with the orthodox concept of economic efficiency, and which he refers to as 'S-efficiency'. Although the workings of market economies have led to an increase in quality of life for much of the world, they have done so at a high cost in resources and have thus tended to decrease S-efficiency. We have now reached the point where, because resources are finite, increases in well-being must be achieved by increases in S-efficiency. Altham gives reasons for thinking that this can be done, and that in this process markets can be our allies.

Toby Lowe's chapter shares some common ground with Shaw, particularly on the conflict between moral values and the tendency of markets to promote self-interested behaviour, but whereas Shaw explores this conflict at the level of individual motivation, Lowe is more concerned with the character of a moral community. He defines a 'community' as a group of people who intersubjectively share identity-forming narratives, and on the strength of this definition he argues that market relations tend to be destructive of community. They subordinate our relations with others to instrumental ones. They undermine the shared narratives which would enable individuals collectively to shape their lives and circumstances. To the extent that market relations have any moral content, they foster only a limited range of values (such as honesty, reliability and fairness). Lowe assesses the claim that market relations leave space for the voluntary moral choices of individuals, and (like other chapters later in the book) he looks particularly at the scope for 'ethical consumers', but he suggests that the fragmentation created by market relations tends to undermine the sharing of experience and of common narratives which are needed to support the choices of ethical consumers.

In Part II we turn to some more specific social contexts in which these potential conflicts between markets and moral values are played out. Barbara Goodwin begins her chapter by reviewing some of the same general arguments as those of Lowe for thinking that the values of business are confined to a narrow range such as those of fairness and honesty and playing by the rules, and that markets may not therefore be suitable providers of public welfare-related services, where other values are needed. She then draws on her own empirical studies of public-sector organisations which have been privatised to suggest that much of the so-called 'public service ethos' may survive privatisation, though reformulated in the language of 'customer service'. She nevertheless suggests that the provision of certain kinds of public services by market institutions is intrinsically liable to be ethically problematic. Customers who are not in any real sense customers (such as benefits claimants), or who cannot help being customers (such as consumers of water) are vulnerable because in that context they are powerless.

Plant suggested that markets have outcomes which can be criticised from the standpoint of social justice. The question of social justice is taken up by Phillip Cole and by David Merrill. Cole's particular concern is with the conceptualisation of poverty, and with the contrast between the 'underclass' conception of poverty and that of poverty as 'social exclusion'. The former conception tends to see the underclass as agents who are at least to some

3

extent responsible for their own poverty, whereas the idea of 'social exclusion' tends to see poverty as the overwhelming of individuals by market forces. The danger of the latter conception is that it tends to view the poor as passive victims of social structures, whereas Cole thinks it important to retain the recognition that they are also at least potentially agents in their own lives. He therefore wants to emphasise that what the poor are excluded from, above all, is power, and what the radical response to poverty stresses above all is the need for empowerment. Where Goodwin has focused especially on those who lack power as consumers of market-provided services, Cole focuses on those who lack power in the labour market.

Merrill notes the failure of contemporary theories of justice to address the workings of the market as an ethical issue. He illustrate this failure through an examination of John Rawls' theory of justice. Rawls' account of the implications of his second main principle of justice, the 'difference principle', presupposes not only perfect competition in a market economy, but a particular conception of the competitive market, which Merrill referes to as an 'end-state' rather than a 'process' conception. Merrill claims that the 'end-state' conception is an artificial construct created by economists for theoretical purposes, rather than one which can apply to the workings of a real economy. A more realistic conception of a competitive economy would have to be allied with a stronger notion of equality of opportunity than Rawls employs, in order to prevent morally arbitrary factors from affecting outcomes in the market. In particular, Merrill suggests, a more adequate notion of equality of opportunity may have to include government intervention to remedy the problem of unemployment and enable individuals to participate in the economy.

The final two chapters return us to questions about the role of the consumer. C.R.E.H. Descombes addresses the question of market relations within the health service, and suggests that the model of the recipient of health care as a market consumer may have a good deal to commend it. The traditional image of the patient suggests a paternalistic relationship in which the patient is passive and compliant. She examines an alternative model, that of the recipient of health care as active 'citizen', but argues that in practice citizens pressing their demands on the NHS are unlikely to match the ideal model of a citizen devoted to the good of the wider community. A more realistic model is that of the consumer, who need not be selfish and irresponsible. The consumer activist of the 'ethical consumer' movement provides a good model for the kind of consumer who will use the health service responsibly.

The 'ethical consumer', whose decisions in the market reflect ethical concerns about, for example, global justice and poverty, or animal rights, or environmental protection, is the topic of Terry Newholm's chapter. He argues that the model of the consumer within the ideology of market liberalism fails to match the reality of ethical consumerism. Ethical consumers are not merely self-interested, and their activity is not that of isolated individuals. They are, and see themselves as, located within social movements, drawing on collective narratives. Newholm thus disagrees both with those who seek to appropriate ethical consumers for market liberalism, and those who criticise ethical consumerism as a conservative acquiescence in consumer capitalism. Ethical consumerism can be located 'between right and left'. It offers a moral critique of capitalism but is reformist in its practice, accepting that we will be living in a market economy for the foreseeable future.

In the light of these chapters can we (to use a suitably market-based metaphor) draw up some kind of balance sheet? Our authors have contended that markets, despite their capacity to promote economic growth and innovation, are morally problematic on a number of fronts. They foster attitudes of self-interest. They tend to commodify values, reducing them to subjective preferences. Though 'efficient' in the economists' narrow sense, they are inefficient from a broader perspective which measures the use of resources to promote quality of life. They fragment social life, undermining people's ability to make moral decisions on the basis of shared narrative understandings. They may be inappropriate mechanisms to deliver certain kinds of public services. They have outcomes which can be criticised from the standpoint of social justice.

What of the possible moral responses which our authors offer to counter these problems? There is, most prominently, the potential of the responsible and informed consumer - the 'ethical consumer' - who can make choices in the market without being dominated by market values. Descombes, Goodwin, Altham, and Newholm, in varying degrees, see some grounds for optimism on this score. Newholm maintains however that ethical consumers have to be envisaged not as isolated individuals but as agents located within social movements and drawing on shared narratives, and that ethical consumerism is only possible in such a context, and we should then bear in mind Lowe's warnings about the propensity of markets to fragment moral communities and shared moral understandings.

The other important category of measures which some of our authors have envisaged to counter the negative moral implications of markets are measures of social justice. A fundamental injustice in market economies is the exclusion of people from the labour market. Merrill refers to the case, based on the principle of equal opportunity, for public intervention to tackle unemployment and enable excluded individuals to participate in the economy. More radically, Cole argues that the response to poverty and social exclusion should be policies intended to facilitate not just participation, but *empowerment* in the labour market. Plant and Goodwin have also commented on problems of power and empowerment. How market relations can co-exist with radical shifts in the distribution of social power is - in this editor's opinion - a question to which no one yet has an answer.

PART I
THE MARKET AND
VALUES

1 The Moral Boundaries of Markets

RAYMOND PLANT

On 23rd July 1997, M. Jospin the French Prime Minister made a speech in London in which he said that he was in favour of a market economy but not a market society. In saying this he encapsulated the beliefs of many. On the one hand the market economy is absolutely indispensable as an engine of economic growth and dynamism; on the other hand the unrestrained market has an inner logic such that market values and market motivation can come to dominate the rest of society and displace other sorts of values and indeed institutions which have their roots in beliefs and attitudes which are sharply distinguished from the market. In this chapter I shall consider what might be regarded as the moral limits of markets. As with most institutions, the very legitimacy of the market may well depend on recognising that markets have to operate within certain boundaries and that they will lose their legitimacy if they operate beyond those limits.

In the 1970s in the United Kingdom the theory of government overload was popular. The claim was made that the British government had lost some of its authority because, since the Second World War, its role and functions had been extended into areas that were not of central concern to government and in which its competence was limited and the risk of government failure was very high. Part of the programme of Mrs Thatcher was to increase the legitimacy of government by narrowing its scope and increasing its authority in a narrower area. Whether this project was successful is not a matter for discussion here. What I am suggesting, however, is that something similar could happen in the case of markets. If markets and the motivations which markets rely on are extended to more and more spheres of life in an uncritical way, then it is possible that they too could come to lose legitimacy, even in areas where they are appropriate. This paper should not, therefore, be construed as an anti-market one. Rather, I am concerned with making sure that the market, which has an absolutely necessary function in a dynamic and pluralistic society, does not jeopardize people's loyalty by being continually extended into areas in which its legitimacy might be questionable.

I believe that it is possible to identify three sorts of moral boundaries to markets. There may, of course, be more, but quite a lot is caught by the following: the moral *underpinnings* of markets, which would not be subject to market activity; what I shall call - following Michael Walzer's argument in *Spheres of Justice*[1] - the moral boundaries to the *sphere* of markets; and the moral *consequences* of markets.

Moral Underpinnings

In talking of the moral underpinnings of markets, I have in mind the idea that in order to work effectively the market requires certain moral attitudes on the part of those involved, and that there is some danger of these moral underpinnings being disturbed by markets themselves, thereby striking at the roots of their own effectiveness and efficiency. I shall discuss two examples of this, although no doubt there are others.

The first is that, although market relations undoubtedly rest upon self-interest, they equally rest upon contract; and contractual relations in turn depend upon a set of indispensable moral attitudes of trust, promise-keeping, truth-telling and taking-one's-word-as-one's-bond. As Emile Durkheim, the French sociologist, once pointed out, 'all that is in the contract is not contractual'. That is to say, for contractual relations to work effectively, there has to be in place a set of moral attitudes and relationships that underpin contract. These, as much as self-interest and enterprise, are necessary conditions of the market order. If morality comes to be seen as a form of self-interest, then it is possible that these moral factors may come to be put into the pot of self-interested calculation; and this would be disastrous for the market itself. If the culture of society comes to be dominated by self-interested conceptions of morality, and business relationships turn into a wholly buccaneering, enterprising sort, then there is at least some danger - if there is no other countervailing set of moral values not based upon self-interest - that the moral assumptions on which the market exchange rests could, in fact, be eroded by a culture of self-interest.

This is an issue which goes back a long way in western history. Some sophists in ancient Greece argued that morality is a matter of self-interest, and that it would be foolish to attempt to act justly if one could get away with acting unjustly when it was in one's interests to do so. Many thinkers on both

10

the Left and the Right of the political spectrum have argued that the capitalist system emerged from within an inherited moral tradition, which protected moral values from the adverse effects of self-interest. However, with the growth of secularization, which is closely related to the growth of the capitalist economy, these values of trust, truth-telling and promise-keeping have been eroded, turning our understanding of morality into one of self-interest. In these circumstances, the moral framework of values - on which capitalism has historically drawn to preserve the values that are essential to its own effective conduct - has become eroded by the very development of capitalism itself.

No doubt the maintenance of these values could be turned into a formal legal matter, so that there could be legal sanctions against a failure to keep to these moral assumptions. However, if these are turned into matters of self-interest, then the authority of law which seeks to preserve values that have a different basis might be undermined. This has become clear recently in the context of the regulation of financial markets. Some defenders of the market have been uneasy about some of these forms of regulation, because they see them as embodying the idea of victimless crime, in which someone can be guilty of an offence caused by the unrestrained pursuit of self-interest without there being an identifiable victim of this self-interested activity.

What seems to be lacking in such complaints is that the integrity of the market can itself be a victim of self-interest if it is not constrained by regulation of this sort. However, if the idea of these being victimless crimes were taken as a reason for easing such regulation, then the point I made earlier would become salient: that is, that the law in this area falls victim to the power of a self-interested view of the nature of morality, in which the maintenance of the integrity of the market itself, as opposed to protecting identifiable victims, is not seen as an important issue. The law can maintain this kind of function only if it is assumed that there is a general morality relating to the market, which has to be preserved. If, however, there is a sufficient change of attitude, so that all that counts is whether someone else's self-interest - the identifiable victim's - has been harmed, then it is difficult to obtain much social consent for having laws that protect some idea of the general moral integrity of the market.

In order to secure such consent, there has to be some wider appreciation of the moral integrity of the market. Of course, it might be argued that this could still make sense in terms of the long-term interest of those involved in market transactions or, alternatively, appealing to some kind of idea of 'universalizability' which would issue in the reflection: what would be the consequences for the market if everyone behaved like that? However, both of these strategies based upon self-interest still presuppose that there is some constraint on self-interest in market transactions, either of a long-term sort, or of a 'universalizable' sort. The potential problem is, though, that the prospects of short-term gains might well override such constraints unless there is some deeper-seated morality in society: what Hegel called *Sittlichkeit*, or 'ethical life' or 'civic virtue', which acts as a countervailing power to self-interest. I shall return to the problem shortly.

The second problem involved in turning these ethical matters into formal ones of legal sanction is that it is more costly and inefficient. If there are internalized values of a non-self-interested kind, which constrain behaviour in the market, then it is at least arguable that this is a less costly form of regulation than what would otherwise be a growing problem, requiring more and more regulation.

The second aspect of the moral underpinning of the market is in many ways parallel to the first, and was well-recognized by Adam Smith: that is, the maintenance of some sense of civic virtue and social obligation in relation to the market. On a purely self-interested view of the morality of the market, attitudes could arise in relation to economic behaviour that actually damage the market.

This could occur in two ways. First, on a self-interest view there would be every incentive for the trader to seek to secure a monopoly in the goods and services that he or she has to sell. Monopolies, again, are harmful to the free market, and also in some cases (such as newspapers and media) harmful to society as a whole. But what argument could be put to a trader that he or she should not try to secure a monopoly if it is in his or her interests to do so? Again, the only appeal would be to some sense of the integrity of the market as a whole, or to a principle of universalizability, or to Adam Smith's own 'impartial spectator' theory: 'What if everyone behaved in that way?'

Again however, this means that there has to be some constraint on self-interest, and this sense of constraint has to be there to support legal sanctions against monopoly. Without some sense of civic virtue, or orientation to values that are not of a self-regarding kind, market behaviour will require growing regulation in the interests of the market itself. This point is well argued by Robert A. Dahl in *Dilemmas of Pluralist Democracy*.[2] Such regulation, in turn, may become increasingly problematic if there is not some more general concern to cultivate a sense of social and civic responsibility, which, as I have suggested, may become more and more difficult with the erosion of social values in favour of private and self-interested ones.

The second way in which this occurs is similar to the first: that is, from the point of view of self-interest, the individual trader may, in a wholly rational way, be a rent-seeker from the government - seeking, that is, to secure privileges from government in terms of subsidies, tariffs or legal privileges. On a free market view these are, again, harmful to the market, and the government has to resist them. However, the same problem occurs again. The state has to act to resist this in terms of the integrity of the market, and in terms of a sense of fairness and justice in the society as a whole. In order to do so, it has to be able to appeal to a sense of civic virtue and consciousness which goes beyond self-interest. Yet the growing role of market relations in society may erode society's capacity to take the steps necessary to protect and reproduce the forms of virtue on which the market rests.

In this sense, therefore, I want to argue that the market certainly requires a sense of enterprise and self-interest, but it equally requires a sense of civic virtue without which the market itself cannot function effectively. The difficulty is that the growth of market relationships may gradually displace those forms of civic virtue and responsibility which, if they were internalized, could constrain individual behaviour in the interest of the market in an informal way; and may, in the longer term, erode the social basis of consent necessary for formal legal regulation when informal mechanisms have failed.

It has been argued that it is possible to reconstruct traditional ideas about civic virtue in terms which depend not upon a traditional or religious framework which, in any case, may be eroded by capitalism, but by developing a moral theory based upon self-interest which, when coupled with some propositions from the theory of games, could in fact enable us to construct a rational morality. There are some exceedingly complex issues allotted to this proposal, not the least of which is how such a theoretically constructed morality could relate to ordinary everyday moral views and moral choices. There are however, in addition, very considerable theoretical difficulties associated with rebuilding ideas such as trust out of premises which depend purely on self-interest. The best explanation of these difficulties is to be found in *Trust Within Reason* by Martin Hollis.[3]

The Sphere of the Market

I now want to turn to a different set of moral boundaries which might be encapsulated in the idea that the market does have a clear sphere, but that

13

equally there are spheres in which market relationships are inappropriate; and that the market may damage its legitimacy in its own sphere if it transgresses those boundaries. The point at stake here is well described by Michael Walzer when he argues as follows in *Spheres of Justice*:

> One can conceive the market [if one is not careful, that is] as a sphere without boundaries, an unzoned city - for money is insidious and market relations are expansive. A radically *laissez-faire* economy would be like a totalitarian state, invading every other sphere, dominating every other distributive process. It would transform every social good into a commodity. This is market imperialism.[4]

Michael Walzer argues that goods and services in society have a social meaning and identity which are closely related to the culture of the society, and which must play a central part in deciding how these goods are to be distributed in that society: for example, whether they are to be distributed by markets, the state, or various kinds of voluntary associations.

I shall take two examples, which clearly imply some kind of dispute about the moral boundaries of the market. These boundaries are not fixed in some kind of theoretical or *a priori* way, but have to be seen to be closely woven into the culture of a particular society. The first example is whether the sale of human organs should be permitted: that is, whether there should be a market in bodily parts. On a strictly capitalist view of market principles, it is very difficult to see why there should not be such a market. The scope for a market is clearly quite wide. There could be a market in blood and blood-products; in kidneys; in sperm; in renting out a uterus for surrogate pregnancy; and so forth.

On a market view, at least three principles would favour a market in these areas. The first is that there is a clear demand for these organs among people who might be in quite desperate need of them. Secondly, the donor system that currently operates may lead to a shortfall in supply, as has certainly happened in the case of kidneys. Finally, if markets are usually construed as exchanges in property rights, then if a person owns anything, he or she owns the parts of his or her body. Indeed, most capitalist theories of property rights - from John Locke to Robert Nozick in his book *Anarchy, State and Utopia* - follow from the idea of self-ownership.

The case for a market in organs and tissues has been put forcefully by advocates of the free market. The Institute of Economic Affairs has long argued for a free market in blood products, to run alongside the donor system;

Woodrow Wyatt argued the case in *The Times* (September 1989) when the issue of the sale of kidneys for the transplant operation in the London Humana hospital was in the news; and Simon Rottenberg , the free market economist, published a chapter called 'The production and exchange of used body parts' in the *Festschrift for Ludwig von Mises*.[5] All of these would see a clear role for markets, and for enterprise and entrepreneurship, in these fields. However, within our society, such advocacy has fallen on stony ground, and I think that most people would feel that some kind of moral boundary had been crossed by the market and the enterprise culture if they could be extended into such fields.

In his well-known book on the blood donor system in Britain, *The Gift Relationship*, Richard Titmuss argued that if blood could be bought and sold, then anything could be.[6] If human tissue is a marketable commodity, then there are really no social limits to 'commodification' and the scope for the enterprise culture. This seems to be a clear case, to use Walzer's terminology, in which the market would be crossing into an inappropriate sphere. This is not because one has to believe in a view that these goods have some kind of essential or eternal nature, to be known and understood on religious or philosophical grounds, which makes it inappropriate for such goods to be treated as commodities and subject to market change. Rather the difference is rooted in the social meaning which goods carry, and these social meanings are part of the cultural and social inheritance of particular societies and ways of life.

We might, of course, want to see whether this social understanding is based upon some clear principle, and this might be important in trying to determine a general limit to the kinds of goods that are subject to commodification. One possibility for a general principle might be an underlying attachment to the idea of respect for persons: that people should not treat themselves as commodities, or as a means to the ends of others. This was certainly the basis of Kant's objection, when he discussed this issue in the eighteenth century in relation to the sale of teeth, hair, and sexuality through the recruitment of *castrati* for the Vatican choirs - although the issues here would also have a bearing on matters such as pornography and the general 'commodification' of the body, and also on the general issue of a market in health care, which makes money-plus-need the criterion of receiving care, rather than just need alone.

It may be that we do not have a consistent view of the moral boundary here. However, for present purposes, all that needs to be said is that the rejection of the sale of tissues and organs implies that there is a deep-seated

15

moral boundary to at least some forms of bodily 'commodification', and that this sets a clear boundary both to markets and to the enterprise culture. It may well be in the interests of the market that this boundary be maintained, for, as I have argued earlier, the market itself has to operate within a framework of moral principle if it is to be legitimate.

The second example of a similar sort is a complex one with many ramifications, which I cannot discuss in detail, but it is concerned with the way in which the extension of the market can displace the service ethic in society. In the view of many free-marketeers, the service ethic in the public sector in spheres such as health care, social work and education is something of a myth. The 'public choice' school of economists argues that those who work in government and health and educational bureaucracies in the public sector are, in fact, motivated in the same way as people in markets. The fact that someone earns his or her living as a doctor, nurse, social worker or teacher does not mean that they have stepped into some new moral realm in which they are motivated by the ethical demands of caring, service and vocation, unlike people in markets who seek to maximize their utilities. They do, in fact, seek to maximize their utilities by using their role in the public sector to increase their responsibilities, the scope of their bureaucracy, their status and their income; and they do this free from the threat of bankruptcy, and in ways that make it difficult for elected representatives to constrain their behaviour because of their professional knowledge and expertise.

Given this diagnosis, there is a case for either privatizing public services and subjecting them to market constraints, or invoking market principles within the public sector by mechanisms such as internal markets - or, if these solutions are not available, for tying providers down by performance indicators and greater specification through contracts and the like, to more definite and less discretionary forms of delivery. If people are motivated by utility maximization rather than the service ethic, then, the argument runs, they have to be constrained by market or quasi-market mechanisms. The caring professions should be demythologized into producer interest-groups, and their behaviour constrained in the same way as behaviour in the market is constrained by the customer.

This argument has many important aspects that cannot be discussed here. However, I do want to question one basic assumption which seems to be involved in this analysis, which implies that the service ethic can be a feature only of voluntary organizations, in which people are not paid and therefore have no incentive to turn themselves into producer interest-groups as maintained by the 'public choice' model. This analysis turns on accepting the argument that utility maximization is the basic form of human behaviour, or at least of behaviour for which one is paid. This assumption is, in itself, highly disputable; and I have suggested earlier that if it is accepted then some assumptions about civic virtue, which may be absolutely necessary to the market itself, are put into jeopardy.

It can also lead to some changes in behaviour among those in the public sector which might, paradoxically, harm the service offered to the client, patient or customer, for if the service ethic is displaced by a contractual or a market one, there is a danger that people whose self-understanding is that they are offering a service, but are being constrained to behave as if they were in a market or a quasi-market, might then act only within the terms of the contract. This has, I think, already happened in schools in the UK. In my experience, there is a strong feeling among teachers that, if they are being put into this kind position, then they will do what their contract specifies but nothing else. It would not then be open to government to appeal to an ethic of service to provide more than is specified in the contract, since the whole point has been to displace the ethic of service and replace it by contract or quasi-market relations.

Again, a market-oriented approach may lead to effects that are unintended. Can we in fact manage a society in which the ethic of service is displaced to the voluntary sector? Just as in the market, where appeal is made to virtues which may not be subsumable under those of private utility and private interests, so too in the state sector the introduction of markets, quasi-markets and the dominance of contract might well deprive us of ethical principles such as service and vocation which are essential to the efficient delivery of services. We have to be very careful about the market again crossing an important moral barrier and replacing one ethic by another. There is another deep issue here. In the public sector, which is part of government and should therefore be subject to the rule of law, we are concerned with things such as equity and treating like cases in like manner. These are not values served by markets, and there is no particular reason why they should be. However, they are central to government and to the rule of law. There is a clear danger that the introduction of market principles into the public sector might undermine these basic principles of public provision and, again, this provides some basic idea of moral restraint on what the role of the market might be in this context.

I now want to turn to another aspect of the sphere of the market, namely its potential influence on how we understand values and their impact on human relationships. I have stressed the idea of potentially unlimited

17

commodification in a market. When goods are turned into commodities to be produced and traded in a market two other things naturally follow: first, such goods are seen as matters of consumer preference and such preferences are rightly seen as subjective; secondly, the pursuit of such goods in the market is explicable largely in terms of self-interest. The danger with the first of those consequences is, I believe, difficult to overstate if we do not see the market as having clear limits. Many people in the UK are concerned about the decline in any sense of public or collective morality which could underpin ideas like civic virtue and common obligation which we should hold together if we are to be good citizens.

In the sphere of commodities and markets the goods in question are assumed to be a matter of individual choice and preference. The value that a commodity has, or its price, is fixed by the individual preferences which individuals have for such goods. That is to say, the value put on them is purely subjective. The transformation of more and more goods into commodities will inexorably lead to these other goods being valued in the same way. As more and more goods are turned into matters of subjective preference, the idea that we do have common obligations and a framework of common morality which has to be sustained if we are to survive as a civilised society is bound to be eroded. The more the idea takes hold that all goods are to be seen as commodities and thus a matter purely of individual value, the less compelling will be the complementary idea that we need to secure a set of common moral values independent of individual choice. We cannot assume that the extension of the sphere of commodities and individual choice will have no impact at all on general conceptions of morality.

Let me take just one specific example which is much exercising policy makers at the moment. The good of sexual relations, and commitment to children as the product of such relationships, has for many men particularly become detached from the obligation to be committed to child rearing and sustaining. So for example Norman Dennis, an ethical socialist, argues in a paper published by the Institute of Economic Affairs (a British free market think tank) that young men have been released from the expectation and requirement that they should make a permanent home with their children and the mother of their children whether it suited them or not.[7] Dennis sees this as part of a general cultural shift from cultural control to individual licence which he says is the most striking and important change of the past forty years.

If we accept this, we shall need a strong sense of moral obligation for public policy to draw upon to change things, and what I am arguing at the

18

moment is that we do need to detach some human goods (including family life and sexual relations) from the idea that all values are subjective matters of preference. This idea is encouraged by the over-colonisation of social life and civil society by market ideas, which assume that so far as the market sphere is concerned all goods are matters of subjective preference. If one looks at the ways in which the market order is justified by many of its most distinguished defenders - for example the Nobel prize winners Hayek, Friedman and Buchanan - the market is seen as the institutional embodiment of value subjectivism. In so far as this is true we should not be surprised that the growing extension of the market order will have an impact on how we conceive value in other aspects of our lives.

The same is true of the other aspects of commodities and markets that I mentioned, namely the way in which they trade upon and engage the motive of self-interest. Now of course it would be naive and silly to deny the role of self-interest in our lives, and markets naturally and rightly engage that aspect of human motivation. Again however, I want to draw attention to the fact that the continuous extension of the market will engage these motivations in more and more areas of our lives and may well, to use one of the marketeer's own phrases, "crowd out" the ways in which we pursue and engage with other sorts of human goods.

Consider again Norman Dennis's point about home making and child rearing. If we live in a world where the worthwhile things in human life are seen to be secured only by self-interest, then we shall arrive at the position which he identifies, namely that people will not be involved in child rearing unless it suits their self-interest to do so. The difficulty is for the state and public policy to alter this if we assume the two things that I have been dwelling on, namely that value is entirely subjective and that preferences are driven entirely by self-interest. To counteract these cultural changes the state can only act if it draws upon a well of moral values and assumptions which point in the opposite direction, but these common values are in danger of being eroded by the continuous colonisation of markets and their associated ideas into the culture of society generally. If we are to restore a sense of obligation both within the private sphere and the public sphere, we need some preserved sense of value which is independent of the subjectivity of value and of self-interest seen in the most short term sense.

There is a further issue here in the context of the impact of the market on other values in society. The dominant image of human relations within the market order is that of contract and this is how it should be within the market order because, as I have argued, goods traded on the market are valued subjectively and self-interestedly pursued, and the purchase and consumption of such goods depends upon contract whether explicit or implicit. A contract is negotiated by self-interested individuals to maximise the self-interest of each in the particular situation in which they find themselves, and the dominant method of arriving at a contract, naturally enough, is not by invoking moral principles but through bargaining. If the market spreads to more and more areas of our lives, then again contract and bargaining will become the dominating motifs of human relationships. If we go down this road the relationships which hitherto we might have wanted to understand in other terms - love, commitment, loyalty etc. - may come to be understood in these terms of bargaining and contract and, if this happens, then again a sphere of human goods conceived in the ways I have suggested will become eroded. So, for example, marriage will come to be seen in predominantly contractual terms, as indeed often happens in the USA, where pre-nuptial contracts are quite common, that is to say, contracts before marriage on how to share the common goods created by the marriage in the event of breakdown.

In *The Philosophy of Right* Hegel saw this as a possibility of modernity: that human relations would be driven more and more to the contractual model.[8] He thought it important to preserve what he called "the realm of piety", by which he did not mean specifically the religious realm, although it would include that for those attached to religious values. Rather he meant the realm which I have just mentioned of loyalty, commitment, love, common obligation, civic virtue and so forth. If we are to preserve our own local realm of piety we need to secure a sense of a set of values and relationships which are made as far as possible immune from the pursuit of self-interest, subjectivity, bargaining and contract.

Moral Consequences

The final sort of limit to markets that I want to discuss is in terms of outcomes. To what extent are the outcomes of economic exchange to be accepted as morally legitimate as they stand, whatever the degree of inequality to which they give rise, whether that inequality is for individuals or groups? Here the free market position has three main arguments at its disposal to support the claim that the outcomes of markets are not subject to a moral critique that could entail redistribution in the interests of social justice and greater equality. The first is that market outcomes are the consequence of individual acts of free exchange. If each individual transaction is uncoerced, then the outcome is procedurally just, being the aggregate result of individual acts of free exchange. Given that its consequences are arrived at freely, there is no case for criticizing the market. Adherence to a just procedure, the market, cannot yield unjust results.

The second argument is that injustice can only be caused by intentional action. We do not attribute injustice to the results of unintended processes. However, a market is an unintended process in the appropriate sense. In a market, millions of people buy and sell whatever they have to exchange, and no doubt this individual buying and selling is undertaken intentionally. The 'distribution' of income and wealth arising from all these individual intentional acts is not itself intended by anyone. Since the distribution of income is not intended, it is by the same token not unjust, whatever its degree of inequality.

The third argument is that, even if there were a moral case for criticizing the market in the interests of distributive justice, we have no agreed criteria of distributive justice. We live in such a morally diverse and fragmented society that there is not the degree of social consensus to call upon to ground a set of principles of distribution. There are many possible distributive criteria: need, desert, entitlement, the contribution of labour, and so forth. All of these are, to some degree or another, principles of distribution; they are mutually incompatible and we have no resources in terms of social morality to underpin one set of principles compared with another.

Overall, taking these arguments together, market outcomes have to be accepted as being, in principle, unprincipled. In this situation, in which the privatization of morality has gone so far, all we can do is trust the outcome of the market. The market, in effect, embodies subjective wants and preferences, and one's value is not be fixed by political means according to disputed principles of justice, but rather by the subjective preferences and valuations of one's goods and services in the market.

This is a formidable and comprehensive critique of end-state principles, such as social justice, which have usually been seen by social democrats, social liberals and democratic socialists as central to restraints on the capitalist market. The critique is so wide-ranging that I cannot deal with it fully here. However, I will make some skeletal points about each of the three arguments, which might then leave a foothold to develop a critique of market outcomes in these terms.

The argument that market outcomes are the result of individual acts of free exchange depends upon a number of rather large assumptions. The first is to do with property rights. Essentially, a market is about the exchange of property rights: the good that I own I sell in the market for good that you own. If this exchange is to be legitimate, then property titles must be held to be legitimate. To impose a regime of market exchange on wider and wider areas of society on the basis of radical inequality of ownership takes it for granted that the property titles that have led through time to existing inequalities are, in fact, just.

It has often been noted that, although private property ownership lies at the basis of capitalist theories of market exchange, there has really been no widely accepted theory of private ownership, and certainly some of those that have been presented, such as Locke's, Nozick's and Hegel's, have very grave difficulties. Often, as in the work of Hayek, the assumption is made that markets can be legitimately imposed on wide inequalities in property because (a) we have no agreed criteria of distributive justice in terms of which property could be redistributed, and (b) property is probably in the hands of those where it can do the most productive good. The worst-off members of society will be helped by the trickle-down effect of the market more than they will be by redistribution, and if those who hold property hang onto it, then it is likely that this will create more economic dynamism to trickle down to the rest of society.

However, each of these arguments is highly contestable. The first argument assumes the truth of what I have been questioning. We cannot really argue that there cannot be a moral case for looking at property ownership because any moral case will be contested. This is the issue to which an answer is needed, not a reassertion of the argument. The second argument assumes the validity of the trickle-down effect. This is a matter shrouded in empirical controversy and depends a good deal on our understanding of poverty. However, there is a moral and conceptual argument raised by the assertion that the poor will be made better off by the market operating against a background of existing inequality, rather than by any other alternative. Often this point is put in terms of a claim that the market empowers the poor more than political allocations of resources based upon an appeal to social justice. However, this is at best dubious if we take the idea of power seriously.

Certainly, in the sense of 'power over', power is a positional good. That is to say, it is a good the value of which depends on some people not consuming it. The clear characteristic of a positional good is that, if it is equally distributed, its value disappears altogether. This seems to be the case with power in the sense I have defined it. If that is so, then power and empowerment cannot be subject to the trickle-down effect, just because positional goods cannot trickle down without disappearing. In order to empower the powerless, it is necessary to remove some of the power from the powerful. This cannot be done by creating more power to trickle down to the rest of society. The point at stake here is that inequality matters in terms of empowerment and it is far too bland an assumption to make that, if markets are imposed against radical social inequality, somehow the poor will be empowered. This cannot be the case if power is a positional good.

The second set of arguments dealt with the unintended nature of market outcomes and, therefore, the irrelevance of social justice. Let us accept for the sake of argument that market outcomes are unintended. We can then ask the question whether the unintended nature of an outcome makes any difference to whether that outcome can be the subject of a critique in terms of social justice. If outcomes are foreseeable for groups of people, then I believe social justice still has a place. At the level of personal morality it is possible to argue that we bear responsibility for the unintended but foreseeable nature of our actions. If market outcomes for groups of people are foreseeable, such as that those who enter the market with least are likely to leave it with least, then by parity of reasoning we could argue that we bear responsibility for the outcomes of processes which, although they may be unintended, are at least foreseeable. This responsibility for the distributive consequences of foreseeable processes is then to be understood in terms of social justice.

The free market theorist can hardly deny that market outcomes are foreseeable, because if it were not so there would be no basis to argue for the extension of markets. For example, the argument in favour of the deregulation of rent rests upon the assumption that it can be foreseen that this will increase the supply of private accommodation available for rent. The foreseeable consequences of markets lie at the heart of the possibility of a critique of their outcomes and of asserting our collective moral responsibility for them.

The final argument, that we do not have a public morality to underpin distributive justice, is a powerful one and takes us back to the points I made in the section about the moral underpinning of markets. The assumption in that context was that the privatization of morality has gone so far, and the reduction of morality to self-interest has become so entrenched, that it is impossible for us to have a public or civic culture that would allow distributive justice to work in that context. I have already suggested that civic virtue is actually central to markets and their legitimacy, and I believe that moral pluralism can be overdone, and in ways that would not only make social justice problematic, but also the moral assumptions on which markets rest.

All I can say here on this very big topic is that I believe that there are basic needs or, following Rawls, primary goods that we have in common as members of a society such as ours, in the sense that these are goods that we need in order to achieve other sorts of goods. Among these are income, food, shelter, education, health care, and health education, together with the capacity to live a relatively free and autonomous life. These goods cannot be secured to individuals as of right, never mind with some degree of fairness or equality, purely by the market; and there is a role for an appeal to distributive justice in terms of these necessary conditions of human fulfilment. This is quite different from the assumption that all human goods should be distributed according to fixed criteria of social justice, a point that I made when discussing Walzer.

Conclusion

My overall thesis is that we should echo M. Jospin and rejoice in the market economy, but reject the market society. Markets are essential to material prosperity, to adapting to changes in human circumstance, to creating new opportunities for human fulfilment. At the same time, however, it is very important that markets are kept in their place within a robust moral framework which is rooted in and drawn from the cultural, religious and philosophical beliefs which characterise the society with which the market is embedded.

Notes

1   Michael Walzer, *Spheres of Justice* (Blackwell, Oxford, 1983).

2   Robert A. Dahl, *Dilemmas of Pluralist Democracy: Autonomy vs. Control* (Yale University Press, New Haven, 1982).

3   Martin Hollis, *Trust Within Reason* (Cambridge University Press, Cambridge, 1998).

4   Walzer, op.cit., pp. 119-20.

5   S. Rottenberg, 'The Production and Exchange of Used Body Parts', in *Towards Liberty: Festschrift for Ludwig von Mises*, Vol. II, ed. F. A. Harper (The Institute for Human Studies, Merlo Park, California, 1971), pp.322-33.

6   Richard Titmuss, *The Gift Relationship: from Human Blood to Social Policy* (Allen and Unwin, 1970).

7   Norman Dennis and George Erdos, *Families without Fatherhood* (Institute for Economic Affairs, London 1992).

8   G.W.F. Hegel, *Philosophy of Right* (English translation by T.M. Knox, Clarendon Press, Oxford, 1952), para. 163.

2 Markets and Moral Minimalism

PATRICK SHAW

1

It is an old joke that talk of business ethics is a contradiction in terms. But behind the joke there lies a real worry, for business activity can appear to be indifferent or even hostile to a moral viewpoint. Critics often complain that businesses aim simply at making a profit, without regard to wider social considerations. For example, reputable companies invest in countries whose governments repress ethnic minorities, trample upon civil liberties, or pose a threat to peace. They encourage women to feed their babies milk formulas even in circumstances when it is likely to damage the health of their babies. They dump industrial waste without sufficient regard to safety. They knowingly sell expensive and unsuitable insurance policies. In short, the critics say that firms put profits first and do not show a strong enough sense of ethical or social responsibility.

The purpose of this paper is to examine one common response to this criticism. The response is important, because it links up with the classic defence of markets given by Adam Smith. I shall argue that it is not very satisfactory and should not assuage the worries of the critics. This response to the charge of putting profit above moral concerns is nicely expressed by William Baumol:

> If we want business to behave differently from the way it does today we must change the rules of the game so that the behaviour we desire becomes more profitable than the activity patterns we want to modify.[1]

When one thinks about it, this is a very peculiar approach to the problem. Suppose a difficult adolescent were to respond to criticism in a parallel way: 'If you want me to behave differently you must change the rules to make it worth my while to behave how you want me to'. We would rightly be shocked. We expect people to behave well even when it is not in their interests to do so. People who are properly brought up know that behaving well can cost them, and sometimes cost them dearly. By contrast, the businessman is here presented as refusing to consider any argument as to what

26

ought to be done; the sole relevant test is what it pays to do. In effect, the response concedes what the critics commonly claim—that businessmen pursue profits to the exclusion of moral concerns—and goes on to propose that it is up to the rest of society to adjust things so that morally acceptable outcomes are guaranteed. No wider concerns properly devolve upon business agents.

Suppose that in what follows we think of businesses as owned and managed single-handedly, thus prescinding from large problems about how decisions within the firm are made, the responsibilities of employees, and so on. Then the charge to be examined is that the typical entrepreneur will behave, so far as business activities are concerned, like someone who is morally defective, never asking 'Is this right?', but only 'Is this advantageous?'. Businesses will do what is right or decent only so long as it does not cost them.

It might be felt that I have over-egged the pudding a little. After all, in many respects businessmen behave perfectly properly. They do not normally blow up their competitors' factories, while, in many an industry, a handshake is as good as any written contract. So in some respects entrepreneurs behave perfectly well. These examples do not quite address the issue, however, for behaviour which accords with morality may be driven by self-interest. As to the handshake, reneging on such a deal might give a short-term gain but at a heavy cost in forfeited trust, so sticking by a handshake might well be an act of prudence. As to the blowing up of competitors' factories, that is illegal; breaking the law runs the risk of incurring high costs; and the risk might not be worth it. In such a case the rules designed to make good behaviour pay are already in place.

Nevertheless, we may suppose that just like other people entrepreneurs do not obey the law simply from fear of being caught, or stick by their handshakes simply because it would not pay them to renege. Like most other people, they think it is a good thing to obey the law and abide by rituals which cement trust, or they habitually do these things without even thinking about them. It seems implausible to suppose that entrepreneurs will take a purely external, calculating view of whatever they do, even in the line of business.

Yet even if they are not amoralists, businessmen are in a position where any moral scruples they possess are distinctly vulnerable. It is not just the inefficient businessman who suffers from competition. The businessman who spends on the training of the handicapped, for example, 'is likely to find that he, too, is vulnerable to the chiseller without social conscience who, by avoiding such outlays, can supply his outputs more cheaply' (Baumol, p. 49). Here is where the moral vulnerability comes in. As long as the business community simply takes for granted an obligation to outlay a certain rough percentage of their costs on training the handicapped, say, then everyone can behave well out of custom or conviction. As soon as someone works out that this is a cost which can safely be cut, because it is not a legal requirement and customers are not going to boycott his goods if he does it, then other firms will follow suit or go to the wall. Big changes can be driven through in this way. Thus, for example, twenty years ago firms tended to carry labour through downturns in the economy. Then the idea caught on of laying off workers when the going got rough. Giving workers job security changed from being something which good employers did as a matter of course to being a luxury which good employers felt no obligation to afford. Similarly so far as supplying military equipment to brutally repressive regimes is concerned: once some firms show they are prepared to supply the equipment, the others cannot afford to be left out. So we can see the point of the plea that, if we wish firms to pursue certain sorts of behaviour, we should tinker with the rules to make it worth their while to do so.

Entrepreneurs are thus susceptible to a kind of moral minimalism, where moral standards are set by the behaviour of the worst. If anyone is prepared to do it, and the law permits it, and it pays, then others will follow suit. Thus we see how reputable firms can come to justify to themselves acting in ways which are unscrupulous. Thus large firms will often adopt a policy of delaying payments to small suppliers, especially those known to be in financial difficulties. This sort of behaviour provides a sharp contrast with the behaviour of most people acting in a personal capacity, where it is frowned upon to take advantage of people in difficulty. Even if some people are unscrupulous in their day-to-day behaviour, the vast majority do not do likewise. They have different standards, and do not need bribes to abstain from morally dubious behaviour. They refuse to follow suit because they think the behaviour is not right, and even if thereby they miss out on some gains they are prepared to miss out.

What accounts for the difference? In a highly competitive economy, as we have seen, the cost of moral scruples—the cost of *not* being a moral minimalist—is likely to be business extinction. The morally scrupulous go to the wall along with the inefficient and the unlucky. A highly competitive economy enforces moral minimalism by selecting against those with scruples. Outside the business world, thankfully, the costs of having scruples are often not very high. People can stick to their principles and thereby perhaps miss

28

out on some benefits, but without dire consequences. It is the highly competitive nature of a flourishing market which selects for moral minimalism. This is a cost of competition which is often ignored.[2]

2

The response which we are concerned with concedes that entrepreneurs do not show much social conscience in their business activities, but claims that nevertheless socially damaging business activities can be restrained. The trick, we are told, is to adjust the rules governing industries so as to reward businessmen for behaving well and penalize them for behaving badly.[3] Then it will pay entrepreneurs to abide by the new rules. Each can behave responsibly without thereby giving a big advantage to his competitors, and the dangers of morally unscrupulous behaviour can be contained by bringing it about that self-interest and the public interest coincide.

This strategy is, however, not particularly successful. When attempts are made to tighten up the rules governing an industry it turns out that the firms in that industry do what they can to undermine any proposed legislation, rather than welcoming it with open arms. We could try engaging business leaders in helping to design effective controls on their own activities. However, as one defender of this strategy concedes, 'It would ... be unreasonable to expect the representatives of industry to spearhead a drive to impose the costs of public interest programs on themselves' (Baumol, pp. 55-6). From the point of view of the entrepreneur it is better to have no controls; and if controls there must be, it is better to have ineffective than effective ones. In that way any social costs of the industry, in terms of pollution, damage to the environment and so on, are met by society at large rather than by the industry itself. Hence it looks like an empty dream to expect entrepreneurs to co-operate in devising good controls over their activities.

One can go further in this direction. Businessmen are unlikely to wait until they are forced to fight a defensive battle. If they can successfully undermine those who threaten to make trouble for their industry—dig out some shady details of private lives, threaten to bring crippling libel actions, or whatever—there is no reason to think they would not do so. It is to their advantage. Again, there may be good reasons for businessmen from different industries to co-operate against the wider public interest. If, for example, they think they are likely to benefit from the rise of certain politicians or political parties sympathetic to business then one might expect them to do some discreet funding. Of course, some of those in business who provide funding for pro-business political parties might be sincerely convinced that what is

29

good for business is good for us all, but even if they are wrong about that it will be good for business anyway, and so quite a reasonable investment.

The hope must be that at some point businessmen will cast aside their business *personae* and take upon themselves the role of concerned citizens, rather than seeing the concerned citizens as a threat to their profits. But there is not much evidence for this. Witness, for example, the pressure from the oil companies in 1997 which forced President Clinton's backtracking in the global warming debate. Certainly there is a risk that the sort of people which business selects for, and the ways people are habituated to behave in business, will spill over; that not only will industries which are not properly regulated produce some socially bad effects, but businessmen within those industries will strenuously resist any attempts at proper regulation.

3

If amoralism, or at best moral minimalism, is the behaviour characteristic of entrepreneurs, then one would expect the general public to regard markets and entrepreneurs with suspicion or even mild contempt, and one might well expect a good society to be characterized by the predominance of institutions other than competitive markets. Why, if a competitive market tends to be subversive of good behaviour, are people so welcoming of markets?

There is a classic answer to this. *First* the market increases living standards:

> Since the beginning of the industrial revolution it has increased real per capita incomes perhaps twenty-fold, incredible though that may seem. It has doubled and redoubled and redoubled again the energy placed at the service of mankind, and has achieved an increasing productivity of human labour which is astonishing.... (Baumol, p. 45)

Second, selfishness in competition works for the general good:

> The invisible hand does not work by inducing business firms to pursue the goals of society as a matter of conscience and goodwill. Rather, when the rules are designed properly it gives management no other option. (Baumol, p. 49)

So, no matter if the actions of entrepreneurs are greedy, selfish and lacking in moral concern; what they bring about is an increase in basic material goods, a precondition of the masses leading lives which are more than a constant struggle against disease and poverty. This is essentially Adam

Smith's defence of markets, dating back to the eighteenth century. Successful entrepreneurs will be driven by self-interest, without any pretence of aiming at the public good. Yet in a well-run, competitive market good will be achieved despite the fact that nobody aims at it.

Undoubtedly this is a strong defence of markets, but it is also in some ways a strange defence. Essentially it claims that the end justifies the admittedly rather dubious means. An area is permitted in which morality is marginalized, in which successful operators are assumed to be motivated by calculated greed, unhindered by moral scruples. Given this view of things it would not be polite to describe anyone as a born businessman. And given these considerations, it would be no surprise if many idealistic young people want nothing at all to do with a business career, since they would have to be prepared to suppress their consciences in a number of their dealings with other people.

If this defence of markets is to provide an adequate response to the problem of moral minimalism then the hope has to be that the area of unscrupulous behaviour will be confined, that entrepreneurs will see business as a sort of game with its own ethos, a game where one's only aim is to come out on top and the rules are there to be bent, but a game which is not morally contaminating. However, as we saw, the evidence is rather against such optimism. There is a real danger that the business ethic will spill over into social life, a problem which the classic defence of markets does not meet. As businesses become international and more powerful than the governments which are supposed to set the ground rules, then we might well expect it to be very hard indeed to make stick any rules which do not suit the agenda of businesses.

Although Adam Smith was concerned about the moral background in which markets are set, such concerns find little direct counterpart in current debate. There is sometimes some unease amongst the general public, as, for example, in the BSE crisis, that the interests of producers are paramount in driving through changes whose effects are unpredictable. Yet among politicians there is an increasing readiness to accept that what is good for business is good for us all.

Perhaps one reason for this is a growing realization in political circles that the controls over markets are already largely ineffective. The agents of control are national governments and many powerful companies are now multi-national and control bigger budgets than some governments. As it becomes more difficult to exert control, it suits those in government to believe that what is good for business is good for us all. There is an incentive for politicians to suppress any doubts they might have on this score rather than to enter into battles with industry which are unlikely to be won. Politicians who announce a problem and then back out of tackling it appear as weak. So do those who fight and get beaten. It is far easier to pretend there was never a problem in the first place.

4

Aside from these worries about the subordination of the social good to a business agenda, the classic defence of markets carries more force when prevailing income levels are low than when they are high. If people are starving, diseased and ill-clad then they can lead virtuous lives but not *good* lives, in the sense of lives that we would wish on them. Some level of material well-being is important so that people can fulfil their needs, formulate projects and shape their lives. Past a certain point, however, it might be wondered whether a further increase in material well-being is so very important. It is a serious question whether a further doubling of real incomes in the richer parts of the world would really make for happier people or better societies.

Economists nowadays tend not to emphasize such things, arguing that markets give people what they want, and taking it for granted that giving people what they want is a good thing. Whether it is a good thing or not depends on a number of issues, including the following:

(1) Some of the things which people want have spillover costs to others which can be quite significant; for example, motor cars in densely-populated areas, or decibel-rich music centres. It may be better, on balance, if some consumer wants remain largely unfulfilled.

(2) Some wants are for what are termed positional goods. John Maynard Keynes distinguished absolute needs from 'those which are relative in the sense that we feel them only if their satisfaction lifts us above, makes us feel superior to, our fellows'.[4] Greater levels of wealth will not diminish these needs. It is not clear that fulfilling the demand for positional goods always constitutes an overall improvement in the situation, since the feelings of superiority which they bring will entail corresponding feelings of inferiority in others.

(3) The market may run counter to other important wants which people have. Markets are dedicated to responding quickly to wants, as expressed in people's purchases. As wealth grows in a community, it would be reasonable to expect its members to be more concerned with wants which markets do not meet, or meet badly: wanting a gentler pace of life, less noise,

more time with one's family, less brand-conscious children, more security of employment. There has to be a trade-off between market efficiency, which involves responding quickly to consumer wants, and stability of employment or income, which people need in order to plan their lives properly. As wealth grows one might expect that proportionately more consumer spending would be on fairly trivial wants, fashion-driven rather than needs-driven, and that non-market goods would become more important.

5

Keynes looked forward to the time, which he thought would be in the new century, when what he called the economic problem, the struggle for subsistence, would begin to be solved for the whole world. There would be enough affluence to enable labour time to be greatly reduced. As a consequence of this, he said:

> All kinds of social customs and economic practices, affecting the distribution of wealth and economic rewards and penalties, which we now maintain at all costs, however distasteful and unjust they may be in themselves, because they are tremendously useful in promoting the accumulation of capital, we shall then be free, at last, to discard. (Keynes, op. cit., pp. 369-70)

Whether or not his prediction turns out to be correct, Keynes was right, I think, to suggest that the customs and practices surrounding the operation of the market should begin to be questioned as prosperity grows. When the accumulation of capital is paramount it can be argued that giving entrepreneurs a fairly free hand is of benefit to society as a whole. Although at times the costs of economic change and displacement can be enormous, the wealth that markets bring is seen as justifying the process. Change is driven through by the desire for profit, and a keen sense of justice in the entrepreneur is only likely to slow the pace of change. In Smith's words, "We address ourselves not to their humanity but to their self-love".[5] When accumulation is paramount, the standards of behaviour in business are not subject to close scrutiny.

The argument has been that markets are competitive and competitive structures tend to put a downward pressure on standards of behaviour. We would expect this in other areas than markets, and sport is an obvious example. Writing of the recent football World Cup, Ruud Gullit spells out the process by which bad behaviour spreads: 'All this diving and conning of referees comes from South America, and European sides quickly learn, because the manager spells it out in very large letters that if you can't beat

33

them then join them. You can't be a saint out there when other people are successfully winning free kicks against you and getting your players dismissed. You have to do it back ...' (*Observer*, 12/7/1998). Yet the downward process is not inevitable. In some sports, most notably golf and snooker, professional players maintain very high standards of behaviour, often owning up to violations of the rules which no one else has noticed. Clearly, while competition has the potential to drive down standards of behaviour, other factors must be involved in explaining how far it has that effect.

In the case of sport, a strong controlling authority which monitors behaviour and punishes misdeeds is important in holding standards of behaviour high. The governing body is often drawn from professional players and former players. In business events have proceeded differently. The expansion of wealth necessitated a movement away from trade guilds, which restrained the dynamism of markets.[6] The controlling authority is an external one, the state, and entrepreneurs are inclined to see the rules it imposes as a nuisance, as bureaucratic interference, rather than as something which they internalize and to which they are committed.

Keynes's point is that as wealth increases and the economic problem comes closer to being solved it is reasonable to be less tolerant of competitive markets and more ready to interfere with their functioning. I have argued that it may not be so simple. The concentration of capital represents a concentration of power, and where business interests conflict with the wider public interest there is reason to think that businessmen will combine to pursue their own interests. Adam Smith would have expected no less.[7]

Notes

1   W. Baumol, 'Business Responsibility and Economic Behaviour', in E. S. Phelps, ed., *Altruism, Morality and Economic Theory*, (New York, 1975), p. 46.

2   Some caveats are in order. (1) If customers are scrupulous, well-informed and prepared to switch their purchasing habits then entrepreneurs will be less able to cut moral corners. Against this, however, a single unscrupulous operator in a highly competitive market can change things, but it takes a lot of principled consumers to have a countervailing effect. (2) If an entrepreneur can tap a niche market then it may be possible to maintain high standards of business behaviour. But niche markets are by definition small

and not highly competitive. Once competition kicks in the downward pressures can begin to operate.

3   Baumol argues, p. 51, that we should use tax incentives rather than laws in pursuing this end, but his argument for this is not convincing. It is that since society would gain from restricting the unsocial activities of an industry it can afford to give business some incentive to behave better; and that laws need policing, which costs money. But why bribe firms to behave well, even if we can afford to? And any claims of entitlement to incentive payments would also need policing.

4   John Maynard Keynes, *Essays in Persuasion*, (London,1931), p. 365.

5   Adam Smith, *The Wealth of Nations*, ed. E. Cannan (New York, 1937), p. 14.

6   There would be other differences. A controlling authority in a market would have to weigh the general benefits of a piece of unscrupulous behaviour, whereas there are few general benefits in a sportsman behaving badly.

7   My thanks are due to Scott Meikle for helpful comments on an earlier draft.

3 Is the Consumer always Right? Subject-relative Valuations and Inherent Values

THEO VAN WILLIGENBURG

1. Introduction: Consumer Rightness and other Sources of Value

One of the most fascinating mechanisms in economics is the way in which the market can make us all wealthier. Say that I possess a bottle of very good wine, a Chateau Bellevue de Rambaud 1997, and that you offer me money in order to become the owner of this bottle of superb wine. Say that you would be prepared to pay 6 pounds for the bottle, and I decide to sell it to you for 5 pounds. It happened that I had the opportunity to import this wine myself from France for the price of 4 pounds per bottle. If I sell you the bottle for 5 pounds, we will both become richer. I will have earned one pound, and you will have earned one pound, as the bottle is worth to you 6 pounds. By simply exchanging this bottle for some amount of money we have both become wealthier. How is this possible?

It is possible because people value goods and services, but value them differently. There may be all kinds of reasons for this difference, but it makes it profitable for people to exchange goods and services. For me, this bottle of Bordeaux is not worth 5 pounds, either because I am not really fond of Bordeaux wine (actually my favourite wine is Burgundy - that is why I was only prepared to pay 4 pounds per bottle when I purchased this Bordeaux wine in France), or because I have so many bottles of this wine that as a cause of diminishing marginal utility I would be prepared to exchange three bottles of Bordeaux for one bottle of say Rioja Gran Reserva. My desire for a bottle of Bordeaux is not as intense as is your desire, so you are prepared to pay more for it than I paid for the bottle. Both of us will be richer if I sell you the bottle for more than I bought it, and for less than you are prepared to pay for it. Simply because of our different desires we put a different value on things. We translate this value in money terms, and then make an exchange to the profit of both of us.

This mechanism of wealth-production is based on the presupposition that the value of objects and services is dependent on the desires of consumers. Not just individual consumers, but the whole group of them. If everybody longs for Burgundy the price will increase. This will make it attractive for more suppliers to enter the market, which will then moderate prices until an equilibrium is reached and the market-price of a good or service is fixed. The price-mechanism shows that the well functioning market is always right in assigning value to objects and goods. Market-rightness is dependent, however, on consumer-rightness. The rational consumer is never prepared to pay more for something than it is worth to him and this depends on his or her preferences and desires. As far as the value of goods and services is concerned the consumer is always right. Or so it seems. People confer value on things. Something is valuable to the degree that you and I consider it worthwhile, and this is shown for instance by our willingness to pay for it.

Still, we believe that there are other sources of value than consumer-preference. Not only can the consumer be mistaken about what is valuable in the market, we also believe that not all value is dependent on preferences and desires. Something may be valuable even if it is not valued by the critical consumer. Something may have value, even if the market would price it as worthless.

The reason for this is that not everything that is good has its value as a result of the interest of consumers taken in it or, more generally, the desire people have for it. There are things as we say which have inherent value or perhaps even disvalue independent of whether there are persons who prefer or desire it (or hate it). Therefore, something may be good or bad for the consumer, independent of his or her valuing it as such.

I would like to discuss two arguments in favour of the position that it is incorrect to think that things have value only as a result of the interest taken in it or the desire people have for it. I call these the argument from objectivity and the argument from intrinsic value. Though I am in favour of the position that it is incorrect to think that something is valuable to the degree that consumers - you and I - consider it worthwhile and desirable, and though I have a lot of sympathy for both the argument from objectivity and the argument from intrinsic value, I will try to show that these two arguments are only partly correct. My purpose is to correct and complement some of the reasoning that lies behind the two arguments. This will help us in better understanding concepts like 'use value' and 'inherent value' of goods.

2.1 The Argument from Objectivity

The argument from objectivity is splendid in its simplicity and clarity. It says that anyone who thinks that something is valuable because we confer value on it is reversing, turning upside down, what is going on when we value something. We value something because it *is* valuable, rather than just calling valuable those things we care about.[1] This is not a bottle of good wine because I like it, I like it because it is so good. Johann Sebastian Bach is not a superb composer because I admire his work, I admire his music because it is superb. I qualify it as excellent, because it *is* of excellent quality, it is not of excellent quality just because I qualify it as such and desire to listen to it. In finding something of value we have the strong impression that we *respond* to something that is valuable. It is strange to think that the sunset is beautiful because we find it pleasurable. In finding the sunset beautiful we seem to respond to some attribute that we perceive in this event: we *find* it beautiful because it *is* beautiful. If you think that it is beautiful because you experience it as beautiful, you are simply mistaken in your idea of the phenomenology of valuing.

I like this argument from objectivity, but I believe it is only half of the truth. But let me first present the other interesting and powerful argument: the argument from intrinsic value.

2.2 The Argument from Intrinsic Value

The argument from intrinsic value says that anyone who claims that something has its value as a result of the interest consumers take in it is turning everything that we regard as valuable into an *instrument* in the service of preference-satisfaction or the production of pleasurable mental states. Something would be valuable because it serves my pleasure or some other subjective experience. The beauty of the sunset would be derived from its being an instrument to creating pleasurable experiences in me, which amounts to saying that final value is only to be found in this experience.

This is clearly an absurd position, says the argument from intrinsic value. For if anything that counts as (finally) valuable is mental, then we need

38

to relate the value of every good to the contribution this good makes to the (experience of) preference-satisfaction or happiness.This is a result not many of us would endorse, however. We do not believe that all value except the value of some mental state is instrumental. Many things may not be conducive to happiness or preference-satisfaction - may not be in any sense instrumental to pleasurable experiences - but still we value them. This shows - says the argument from intrinsic value - that there are many instrinsic values, many goods valuable as ends in themselves, and not just as means to satisfying the desires of consumers.

The problem with this argument from intrinsic value is, that it does not separate *intrinsic* value from *final* value and, therefore, it concludes that everything that is non-instrumentally, and so finally, good, must be intrinsically good. But this seems to be rather far reaching. I believe that the value of this lovely Bordeaux does not just rest in its usefulness. This is not just useful stuff to slake my thirst, or to make me tipsy which may be a pleasant state to be in. This bottle is not just valuable as a means to cheer up thirsty and slightly depressed people (there are other cheaper means to achieve that). But do we have to believe, then, that this bottle of Bordeaux has intrinsic value of its own? If we are not choosing other means to quench our thirst or become tipsy, is this because of some intrinsic features of this bottle of Bordeaux, features which are valuable on their own, independent of any human desire, interest or concern? What are these intrinsically valuable features and how would we know that they are there?

3. Extrinsic, Final Value

Christine Korsgaard has argued that we have to keep apart two different kinds of distinctions in goodness:[2] the distinction between (1) *intrinsic* and *extrinsic* value on the one hand, and (2) *instrumental* and *final* value on the other. To say that something is intrinsically good is to say that it has its goodness *in itself*, something is extrinsically good if it gets its value *from some other source*. To say that something is instrumentally good means that it is valued *for the sake of something else*, something is good as an end if it is valued *for its own sake*, it is a final good (not valued as a means to something else). To call something instrumentally or finally good is saying something about *the way* we value that thing (as an instrument or as an end). To call something intrinsically or extrinsically valuable is to say something about *the source* of goodness of the thing (where does it get its value from?).

39

I will not fully expound Korsgaard's argument, but use the distinction to make the following point: any value (except the value of human deliberation and agency itself) must be extrinsic value, because it is always value *for us*. Things can only be valuable under the condition that there are people for whom they may be valuable, as only humans have the capacity to confer value on things.[3] Things cannot be unconditionally valuable, they can only be valuable under the condition that people take an interest in them, have a concern for them, deem them valuable etc.[4] In other words, things can only be extrinsically valuable. But this does not mean that that all extrinsic values are instrumental values, as if something is only good under the condition that it serves as an instrument to some end. Yes, instrumental goods are extrinsic goods (in this sense there is a clear connection between the two sorts of value-predicates distinguished). But also non-instrumental goods, that is things of final value, are extrinsic goods; they are valuable as goals in themselves under the condition that they are recognized and valued as such by us. There may, thus, be *extrinsically valuable ends*: non-instrumental goods which are not intrinsically but only conditionally good, the condition being that someone takes an interest in them as valuable for their own sake.

Why are these distinctions so important? Take again the example of a beautiful sunset or a superb work of art. It is hard to defend the claim that such beautiful things are intrinsically, that is unconditionally good. As least as far as sunsets are concerned, we know that there may be conditions under which one comes to hate the sun: say if one lives in Saudi Arabia one will welcome a sunset, but not for its beauty. So the beauty of a sunset is only a good under certain conditions in which people come to admire that beauty. It is not of intrinsic/unconditional value, it is of extrinsic value. But if one equates extrinsic value with instrumental value, one will have to point out some final good that is presumably served by this instrumental value, in order to understand why the beautiful sunset is valuable at all. The only option is that one regards the view of a beautiful sunset as a means to some kind of pleasurable experience in me. Such a subjective position which amounts to the idea that works of art or other aesthetic events are only valuable because they serve my pleasure or some other subjective experience, is - as we have seen - highly counterintuitive. We believe that the beauty of a fine sunset or a good work of art must be final, valued for its own sake.

However, if we try to save this finality, this non-instrumentality of the value of a beautiful sunset, a work of art or bottle of Bordeaux, by equating final value with intrinsic value we have another problem. One will have to allow that this event (the sunset) or this fluid (the Bordeaux wine) has some

40

property which makes it good independently of our valuing it as such, so independent of any interest that we take in it. But this leads to some serious ontological and epistemological problems: how can we assess the value of the event, that is, how can we know that it has this specific property which makes it valuable, independent of our valuing it as such? If the goodness of something only depends on its intrinsic nature, how can we assess this goodness and know that we are justified in valuing it, distinct from this very activity of valuing it? If the goodness of an end is always intrinsic goodness and has nothing to do with the mental attitudes taken towards that end, how do we know that it is good? We will inevitably end up endorsing some sort of hard-to-defend intuitionism: the position that goodness is a metaphysical, simple property that we intuitively perceive in things and to which we in some way respond.[5]

We need not save the finality of goods by looking for some intrinsic, i.e. unconditional quality of those goods. Things may be non-instrumentally, finally good, without being intrinsically good. There are extrinsic final goods: things that are valued for their own sake, but not unconditionally. The condition might be that the things can be *valued* by a person, by a group of persons or by humans as such, that they can be experienced as valuable. This does not mean that final value is to be found in this experience (as if everything good as an end must have something to do with something mental, some kind of experience). But still, the goodness of the thing must have something to do with goodness *for us*. The mistake in equating extrinsicness and instrumentality is that it presupposes that things can only be good for us because of their usefulness. Use-value is certainly always value for somebody. But also aesthetic value is value for us. The beauty of a sunset or a good painting is valuable in itself, but it is only valuable under the condition that there are people who value it.

4. Euthyphro Reconsidered

It will now also be clear why I believe that the argument from objectivity is only half of the truth, and why - for the same reason - the Euthyphro-problem (is something valuable because we *find* it valuable, or do we find it valuable because it is valuable?) is seriously misleading.[6] It tries to separate two things which cannot be taken apart: (1) the fact that a Bordeaux wine is valuable, that it deserves to be valued because of its specific properties, and (2) the fact that this wine merits our valuation because of its value for us, that is given specific human concerns, interests and desires. I find Bordeaux wine valuable because it is valuable, but also it is valuable because I find it valuable - given certain desires, given a social setting that holds up norms for valuing in culinary matters. If there were no people who would be pleased by tasting fermented grape juice, if there were no people who would appreciate the craftsmanship that goes into producing a bottle like this, if there were no people who would admire the nice label on this bottle, it would not be a valuable thing. But that does not mean that value is to be found in the experience of appreciation, the feelings of admiration or the amount of pleasure. Value is to be found in the object of valuation, and therefore, there may be independent criteria for judging whether something really merits our appreciation. But still, a configuration of properties of an object can only be valuable given certain human concerns, interests and desires.[7] Something is only of value under the condition that it (can) be valued by us, i.e. if we would be disposed in specific (ideal) circumstances to respond to it favourably.[8]

Having clarified the idea that all values are always values *for us*, it is now time, however, to say something more about various ways in which values can be values for us. The value of a pleasurable mental state of mine is a value for me, but not in the same way as the value of a beautiful work of art is a value for me. We may distinguish subjective values-for-us from more objective values-for-us. Subjective values are values which are fully defined in terms of the peculiarities of the perspective of a subject. Subjective values are, therefore, *perspectivally variant*. A value is objective if it is possible systematically to transform our judgement concerning that value across different points of view. So an objective value is *systematically invariant*.[9]

My enjoyment of a specific flavour of ice cream is an example of a subjective value, because all we can say about this value is exhausted by my subjective perspective on it. All contents of subjective experiences which are valuable to me are subjectively valuable, as it is not possible to understand the content of the judgement of value independent (or in some way detached) from the subject's grasp of that value. Subjective values are perspectival 'through and through'. Your taste need not be my taste (therefore: de gustibus non est disputandum).

Moral values and also aesthetic values, on the other hand, are understood by most of us as being to a certain degree perspectivally invariant and thus more objective. But this is the same *kind* of objectivity - some philosophers would say - as the objectivity of secondary qualities (colours, smells, sounds).[10] Colours exist independently of us, but still they only exist for people who are not colour-blind. If you are colour blind you will never understand what it means that an object is red (though you may be able to distinguish red objects, because of their specific shade of grey). In order to grasp colours one needs to be endowed with specific epistemic qualities. Moral values and aesthetic values can in the same way be understood as perspective-bound and objective. Moral values can only be grasped if one has specific dispositions to be concerned about the worth and well-being of others and oneself. Aesthetic values can only be grasped if one is in a certain way susceptible to effects of a work of art and has developed some sense of judgement. Still, these values will be objective to the degree that they are to be understood as supervening on constellations of facts independent of us. That means that one's perspective will condition one's access to objective values, but still the judgements concerning those values will be stable across classes of judges, because people are responding to facts independent of them and share standards of practical reasoning which make it possible to provide good (and often conclusive) reasons for thinking that certain constellations of facts *merit* certain responses.[11] That is why moral and aesthetic values will be the same for different agents, no matter how they are located vis-à-vis those values.

5. Mixed Goods

The distinction between the 'subjective' and the 'objective' in terms of (in)variability over perspectives, may help us to understand the mixed origin of the value of a good bottle of Bordeaux wine. There is instrumental value here and final value. The value of such a bottle is instrumental in so far as drinking the bottle will be conducive to slaking my thirst, to putting me in a pleasurable mood as the alcohol level in my blood increases or to my having this enjoyable feeling that I am doing something very luxurious by drinking this wine. This is instrumental value that is conducive to subjective final value.

Still, we believe that the value of the lovely Bordeaux does not just rest in its being instrumental in causing pleasurable mental states which have subjective final value. The bottle seems to have features that are valuable on their own, i.e. it possesses final value that does not rest in mental states. Part of this is surely the aesthetic worth of having such a beautiful bottle with fine wine. This value-in-itself is present in many of the mixed goods we price highly. Why buy silver cutlery if the use-value of good plastic spoons, knives and forks is equal? Why have wine in a bottle with a beautiful label, instead of in a more practical sealable plastic can? The aesthetic and perhaps culinary values embodied in a bottle of good Bordeaux wine are not subjective in the sense of being perspectival through and through (like the enjoyment of drinking wine). These values are perspectivally invariant up to a certain degree. Though aesthetic and culinary values are values for us, they are not dependent on the peculiarities of the various perspectives of each of us. These values may roughly be the same for people with different perspectives and differently located vis-à-vis those values.

We may thus gain a better understanding of the 'use-value' and the 'inherent value' of goods. Many things are inherently good - i.e. finally good, good as an end in itself - without having this goodness reside in features which have value fully independent of human ways of appreciation and concern. Still, these goods may be relatively objective, i.e. perspectivally invariant. Mixed goods are examples of things which have both use-value (conduciveness to preference satisfaction) and inherent value. The example of mixed goods also shows that it is not very helpful to make a clear-cut distinction between market-goods, that is goods which can be commodities in the market because of their use value, and goods which cannot be traded in the market because their value does not reside in the way they are conducive to pleasurable mental states of the consumer. It is not that use-value belongs to the sphere of the market and other value not. Completely useless objects like paintings, antique furniture on which you are not supposed to sit, and even Bordeaux wine from the beginning of this century which can no longer be drunk, are popular objects for trade. And the fact that they are sold and people pay for them does not show that their value is to be found in the contribution they make to the joy and pleasure or more general preference-satisfaction of consumers. If you buy my bottle of Bordeaux wine you have not become richer just because you more strongly enjoy possessing this bottle than possessing five extra pounds. You have become richer because for you the value of this bottle is greater than the use-value of your money. So long as you can make this kind of comparison between the use value of money and the mixed value of a bottle of wine, this bottle is a suitable object for trade. If you know, however, that trying to make this kind of trade-off would in some sense ignore or disrespect the value of a good or service, i.e. it would not do justice to the reasons given by its properties for valuing it, then the good or service would not be an appropriate commodity in the market.

The market has limits, yes, but these limits are not given by the instrumental use versus the inherent value of things. Value is always value for us, but not all values-for-us can be acknowledged in the market, though this does not exclude many goods that are ends in themselves as suitable objects for trade. So in a sense the consumer is always right, in that the value of goods and services will be conditional on certain human concerns, interests, desires and socially established practices of appreciation. But on the other hand, the consumer may be wrong, simply because (s)he may not fully grasp the reasons for valuing an object, i.e. (s)he may not duly estimate the value that in some sense supervenes upon the configuration of properties of that object.

Notes

1   This is the argument with which Socrates in Plato's *Euthyphro* objects to Euthyphro's definition of the pious as what the gods love. According to Socrates, the gods love pious acts because they are pious, rather than acts being pious because they are loved by the gods (*Euthyphro*, 10B-11B). More generally (as the question arises whatever the source of authority is supposed to be): we care about the good because it is good, it is not good because we happen to call it good.

2   Korsgaard, C.M., 'Two Distinctions in Goodness', *The Philosophical Review* 92 (1983), 169-195, reprinted in: Korsgaard, C.M., *Creating the Kingdom of Ends* (Cambridge, Mass., Harvard University Press, 1996), 249-310. Korsgaard's position on the nature and origin of value is well expressed in her *The Sources of Normativity* (Cambridge,Cambridge University Press, 1996).

3   Korsgaard: *humanity* is the only source of value.

4   This is not what Korsgaard would say. According to Korsgaard, the fact that people take an interest in something may only be an occasion to deliberate about it and see whether one could justifiably *judge* the thing to be valuable. The origin of value rests on this moment of judgement in which we express our capacity to reason. See Korsgaard, C.M., *The Sources of Normativity* (Cambridge, Cambridge University Press, 1996), esp. pp. 238-242 and Korsgaard, C.M., *Self-Constitution in the Ethics of Plato and Kant* (1998) manuscript. esp. note 55 (pp. 89-90).

5   This is the implication of G.E. Moore's contention that goodness has nothing to do with our desires, concerns, interests, valuations, beliefs, or any mental attitude that we have towards things. See Moore, G.E., *Principia Ethica* (Cambridge, Cambridge University Press, 1971), and Moore, G.E., 'The Conception of Intrinsic Value' in his *Philosophical Studies* (London, Kegan Paul, 1922).

6   Johnston, M, 'Dispositional Theories of Value', *Proceedings of the Aristotelian Society*, supp. 63 (1989) 139-174, 171 ff. See also note 1.

7   See Wiggins, D., 'A Sensible Subjectivism', in *Needs, Values, Truth*, (Oxford, Blackwell, 1987) 185-214.

8   Lewis, D., 'Dispositional Theories of Value', *Proceedings of the Aristotelian Society*, supp. 63 (1989), 113-137. Johnston, M , 'Dispositional Theories of Value', *Proceedings of the Aristotelian Society*, supp. 63 (1989), 139-174.

9   See Alan Thomas, 'Values, Reasons and Perspectives', *Proceedings of the Aristotelian Society* 97 (1997), 61-80; and also Amartya Sen, 'Positional Objectivity', *Philosophy and Public Affairs* 22 (1993), 127-145; Adrian Moore, 'Points of View', *The Philosophical Quarterly*, (1987), 1-20.

10   See for instance McDowell, J., 'Values and Secondary Qualities', in T. Honderich (ed.), *Morality and Objectivity* (London, Routledge, 1985), 110-129. For a critical survey of the analogy between values and secondary qualities see Blackburn, S., 'Errors and the Phenomenology of Value', in T. Honderich (ed.), *Morality and Objectivity* (London, Routledge, 1985), 1-22 and Wright, C., 'Moral Values, Projection and Secondary Qualities', *Proceedings of the Aristotelian Society*, Supplement 63 (1988), 1-26.

11   My position here is a *dispositionalist* one in the style of Wiggins, D., 'Moral Cognitivism, Moral Relativism and Motivational Moral Beliefs', *Proceedings of the Aristotelian Society* 91 (1991), 61-85, and Johnston, M., 'Dispositional Theories of Value', *Proceedings of the Aristotelian Society*, supp. 63 (1989), 113-137. See also Pettit, P., 'Realism and Response-dependence', *Mind* 100 (1991), 587-626; Brower, B., 'Dispositional Ethical Realism', *Ethics* 103 (1993), 221-250.

4   Quality of Life, Environment and Markets

J.E.J. ALTHAM

1

I start with a quotation:

> The most striking thing about modern industry is that it requires so much and
> accomplishes so little. Modern industry seems to be inefficient to a degree
> that surpasses one's ordinary powers of imagination. Its inefficiency
> therefore remains unnoticed......An industrial system which uses forty per
> cent of the world's primary resources to supply less than six per cent of the
> world's population could be called efficient only if it obtained strikingly
> successful results in terms of human happiness, well-being, culture, peace,
> and harmony. I do not need to dwell on the fact that the American system
> fails to do this, or that there are not the slightest prospects that it could do so
> if only it achieved a higher rate of growth of production, associated, as it
> must be, with an even greater call upon the world's finite resources.[1]

In this passage Schumacher is implicitly rejecting the orthodox concept of
efficiency and replacing it with his own. As a trained economist, he must
have been aware of what he was doing. That he did not explicitly draw
attention to his shift in the meaning of 'efficiency' should be regarded as a
device in the service of a polemic. Economic efficiency in the usual sense is
an amoral concept, although normative conclusions are sometimes drawn
from facts about the extent to which it is realised. Efficiency in this standard
sense in relation to resources is measured by the degree to which they are
allocated to the most highly preferred uses. It can in principle be attained
while well-being and happiness remain at a low level. More generally and
more informally, when we speak of the efficiency of modern economies, we
are often thinking of dynamic aspects. We think, for example, of the speed
of response of economic activity to changes in preferences, and of the rate of
discovery of unsatisfied desires and of innovation to satisfy them.

Schumacher does not here, and does not need to, deny that modern economies (although he writes specifically of 'the American system' the criticism is intended to apply to modern capitalist economies generally) are efficient in these senses. He has in mind another concept that he implicitly takes to be fundamental. It can be arrived at in the following way: ethically, we judge the success of a society by the quality of life enjoyed by its members, in relation to what we think of as possible for that society, given the constraints to which it, and its members, are subject. Members of society are no doubt largely pursuing their personal projects when engaged in economic activity, but we can and do look at the outcome of these manifold individual pursuits as a whole. If we conclude that the quality of life enjoyed by the members of the society is low, we may be prompted to try to find out the reasons for this, and may conclude upon investigation that the institutions of the society are defective, or that many of the activities of its members are misguided, or both. The quality of life of individuals is regarded as the fundamental end of society, and its arrangements, and the activities of the individuals, are judged as though they were means. Individuals do not of course generally conceive their activities as means to the quality of life of society at large, but if a certain activity, even if individually rational, has adverse effects upon general quality of life, it is often reasonable to discourage it on those grounds.

If we take quality of life in some suitably inclusive sense as the fundamental goal of society, then its institutions, laws and other arrangements can be judged by how well they serve this goal. The economy of a society can be thought of, from this point of view, as the set of arrangements for transforming raw materials into quality of life. This yields Schumacher's concept of efficiency. An economy is efficient if the contribution to quality of life made by each unit of resource is as high as possible. In citing happiness, well-being, culture, peace and harmony, he is listing major overlapping components of quality of life, and his claim of inefficiency is that, given the amount of resources consumed *per caput* by modern industrial economies, the quality of life of their members is remarkably low. It should be noted that this does not mean that it is low absolutely, or by historical standards. Quality of life could be higher than ever before, while efficiency declined.

Use of this concept of efficiency may be resisted by some, on the grounds that it might seem to provide justification for authoritarian intervention. Politicians may be tempted to use the notion to repress individual choice in the service of this kind of efficiency. The diagnosis of inefficiency is, however, logically independent of political prescription. Antiauthoritarians can see the argument as addressed to the individuals themselves, who may then, if convinced, change their own lives, and press for change through the democratic process.

Schumacher's notion of efficiency, which I shall refer to from now on as S-efficiency, can usefully be compared with the notion of sustainable economic welfare, an index of which, the ISEW, was devised by Daly and Cobb, and has been further developed and applied by the New Economics Foundation.[2] The ISEW is motivated in part by a sense of the inadequacies of Gross National Product as a measure of how well an economy is doing. For example, depreciation of an asset is intuitively a negative element in economic welfare, but it is *added* to GNP. Expenditures people incur to defend themselves against the bad consequences of other economic activity - such as installing sound insulation against aircraft noise - also detract from welfare, but are counted positively in the calculation of GNP. The ISEW attempts to correct for these and other anomalies, and in particular attempts to take proper account of matters affecting sustainability, such as the rate of depletion of natural assets such as forests.

Now suppose that the ISEW rises as a result of some beneficial and sustainable technological change. Does it follow that the economy has become more S-efficient? It does not. The index may have risen because a new use has been found for a material whose rate of use can be increased without endangering sustainability. For example, if there were a breakthrough in the technology for desalinating sea-water, sustainable economic welfare might well go up. However, this is quite compatible with the application of this new technology being very S-inefficient, as it is plausible to suppose it would be if most of the newly desalinated water was used on golf courses rather than to grow crops in arid areas.

Conversely, sustainable economic welfare might decline while S-efficiency increased. For example, economic welfare might decline as a result of some naturally occurring (as opposed to human induced) adverse environmental change, and there might still be a net decline even if S-efficiency improved.

It remains true that in many circumstances S-efficiency and the ISEW will move more or less together. For example, if people install more draught-proofing and heat insulation in their homes, they get the same level of comfort while spending less on gas. If they spend what they would have spent on gas on sustainable worthwhile items, there is a gain in S-efficiency and in sustainable economic welfare.

These examples, however, fail to bring out a respect in which S-

49

efficiency is radically different from an economic indicator. S-efficiency is attained when each unit of resource contributes as much as possible to the quality of life. There are two fundamentally different ways in which there may be a change in the degree to which it is attained. First, S-efficiency varies depending upon how one pursues a given set of projects, attainment of which is judged to constitute a high quality of life. Secondly, S-efficiency varies with the choice of projects. For example, suppose that at one time Alex has a conception of a high quality of life such that to realise it he must own and use, among many other expensive items, a private jet aircraft. Assume, if only for the sake of the example, that there is nothing false about such a conception, and that its realisation may be pursued more or less S-efficiently. Now suppose that Alex undergoes a large shift in values. He comes to think that what would really make his life go well is to come to understand Plato. Assume, as we may, because we should be pluralists about what constitutes high quality of life, that there is nothing false about this conception either. Its pursuit requires few resources. Alex becomes more S-efficient. His quality of life is as high as before, although his objectives are very different, but he uses far fewer resources in living it.

This example shows how far S-efficiency is from any standard economic concept. There are good reasons why it is not used in economic theory. For one thing, it could not have a place in a strictly positive economics, since it is an explicitly normative notion. Secondly, its application depends upon judgements of quality of life, and upon comparisons of quality of life. These are controversial matters, and the controversy has no foreseeable end. Yet Schumacher was justified in using it, and it is employed, explicitly or implicitly, in a wide range of circumstances. Consider first the environmentalist's slogan 'You can live better on less'. This has more than one interpretation. It may be read as saying that people can realise their *existing* conceptions of well-being with use of fewer resources, but it may also, and more interestingly, be read as claiming that there are other, *improved* conceptions of well-being that can be realised with reduced resources. This latter is ethically one of the most challenging features of environmentalism, that it attempts to develop proposals for human cultures that are not merely sustainable but also genuinely more rewarding for their members than living in accordance with the values of current industrial society.

S-efficiency is used in a simpler way when we recognise that some individuals are better converters of consumption into utility than others. This is a widespread common sense belief. For example, we think of some people as being hard to please. When Norma wants a good dinner, she is happy with Chicken Chow Mein from the local take away; but to make Caroline as satisfied, she must eat at Le Manoir aux Quat'Saisons. Some people get less out of what they consume simply because they have melancholy dispositions. Some have more aesthetic sensitivity than others, and suffer more from the hideous aspects of modern life. Some are better able to insulate themselves from things that naturally cause distress, whether by averting attention or stoicism, or by some special technique. I well remember the envy I felt when, waiting at an airport in my usual state of exasperation, I saw a man in the lotus position, meditating and in a state of apparently complete equanimity. More seriously, we generally think that disabled people need more resources than others to get as much out of life. There are numerous other examples of variations in S-efficiency. The compulsive shopper, attempting to compensate for deficiencies in her emotional life, is an S-inefficient consumer. The company rep who cries when his boss allocates him a Vauxhall instead of the BMW he expected would be more S-efficient if he cared less about status. A sportsman who plays for the camaraderie and for the sake of the personal challenge, has a more S-efficient attitude than the one who competes solely to win.

It is easy for those in the West with average incomes or more to take for granted the particular style of affluent life to which we have become accustomed. Given typical Western preferences and values, for example, it is a real deprivation to be without such things as a colour television and video recorder. The danger is to forget the condition, that the deprivation is relative to certain assumptions about the good life, and to forget that these are neither necessary nor universally shared. If we also believe, as is reasonable, that Western styles of affluence are not universalisable, because the resources of the planet do not permit the whole of the world's population to live like a typical American, European or Japanese, we may be made pessimistic about the future for humanity, and conclude that general well-being is unattainable. Thoreau famously said that the mass of men lead lives of quiet desperation,[3] and it can seem that they must continue to do so. The larger the gap between the material possessions a person considers necessary for a good life and their actual position, the less chance there will typically be of bridging it. If the gap remains despite one's best efforts, the result may well be a failure of hope. Thoreau's life by Walden pond was an experiment to diminish the gap by minimising material necessities. It can be considered an exercise in increasing S-efficiency. Thoreau gives us reason to believe that he enjoyed a high quality of life. We may think that we could not live like that, or that we could, but would hate it, but it can still be claimed that his was *one* way of achieving well-being. The experiment has limited application, since Thoreau was on his own. It would have been different had he had a wife and children. A more recent experiment in achieving S-efficiency is that of Masanobu Fukuoka, who has made the extraordinary claim that a full acre is if anything too large for a family farm.[4] Even allowing for the fact that he is referring to highly productive Japanese land, the claim seems absurd, for he is not thinking of families who cultivate a little land on the side while their members mainly earn their living in the city, as many Japanese do. The idea is rather that the farm is their entire livelihood. Supposing that a family can gain enough for subsistence from an acre, will their lives not be cramped and stunted if this is all they have? Fukuoka denies that they will. They will have the precious resource of *time*, since the acre does not take much labour to cultivate using his methods, and they can use this time for various purposes, and notably to make spiritual progress.

A lengthy discussion would be needed fully to explain and to assess Fukuoka, and this is not the place to do so. The point is rather to claim that our conception of well-being may need to be broad enough to allow that those who live according to his prescriptions may enjoy a high quality of life. An anecdote will also illustrate a similar point. I once heard a talk from a young man about his work among poor people in South America. In due course he was joined by other aid workers. He said of them that there was trouble, because these others received salaries, and that nearly ruined the project. He was impatient to return to where he could again live without a salary and feel fulfilled. Of course there was much that, living near the Amazon, he had no access to. No European high culture - no architectural masterpieces, no art galleries, no libraries, no classical music - and none of the common light entertainments - no pubs, restaurants, cinema, television, magazines and so on. But then he had lived a life he had experienced as of great value, and those who have always lived in the West have not had *that* valuable experience.

In the West, living with few or no possessions has historically been associated with that element in the Christian tradition which emphasises contempt for this world, because this world is a scene of degeneration and sin following the Fall of man, and we must distance ourselves from it and keep our minds on Heaven. This tradition is currently in deep recession. Christians to-day tend to follow a doctrine more friendly towards material accumulation, namely that riches are a sign of God's grace. Non-Christians reject the beliefs that ground *contemptus mundi*, and so have no reason to

52

embrace it. But it would be fallacious to infer from the falsity of Christianity that there are *no* grounds for the idea that a good life does not require much in the way of material possessions. It is possible instead to draw on the Greek tradition. Aristotle,[5] for example, claimed that the most noble limit for possession of external goods was that which enables us to perceive the irrational part of our souls as little as possible. It is plausible that this limit falls at a point where the use of resources is at a modest level.

It is not my intention to offer a materially extremely modest life as a universal model. To do so would be unrealistic and would ignore or undervalue some great achievements that have needed large resource inputs. If one's ethic enjoins the maximisation of well-being as its sole and supreme objective, S-efficiency would be sought everywhere, and many grand projects would be excluded. But the concept of S-efficiency is not the property of any one ethical theory. Any sensible view should have a place for it. If there is enough S-efficiency and it is sufficiently widespread, then the well-being of all can be made compatible with the pursuit of resource-intensive projects by a few.

2

Further light can be shed by developing a conception of well-being which is appropriate to the present context. I give a partial outline that I hope meets the purpose. The conception has three parts, which are as follows, in descending order of importance:

> (1) Well-being requires the satisfaction of the necessary and sufficient conditions for species-typical functioning of a human being. This may be called the *needs* component. It includes such obvious things as nutritionally adequate and uncontaminated food, clean water, shelter, clothing and security.
> (2) Well-being requires opportunities for choice of pursuit among worthwhile goals. Call this the *projects* component.
> (3) Well-being requires opportunities for choice among things merely wanted. For example, I may be able to choose between tea and coffee for breakfast. Neither forms any part of any project of mine, and the choice is in itself a trivial one, but unless I had a reasonable variety of such choices, my well-being would be adversely affected. Call this the *mere desires* component.

The satisfaction of these three requirements of well-being does not guarantee

53

personal happiness. Personal temperament or misfortune, for example, may make somebody unhappy even if all their needs are met, they have worthwhile projects, and choices among desired objects. The three components do however seem to capture the main things that we have in mind when we make overall judgements of a society, for they cover the main aspects that can be affected for better or worse by collective action. It may also be said that, given a normal temperament, someone whose needs are met and who has opportunities of the kind described is likely to be happy for much of the time, with the important proviso that there should not only be opportunities to pursue worthwhile projects, but that those chosen should actually *be* worthwhile.

It is clear that in some societies these three requirements are met with a smaller throughput of resources *per caput* than in others, and that in a given society they are met for some individuals with fewer resources than for others. These facts provide application for the concept of S-efficiency in relation to this conception of well-being.

It is not difficult to see what S-efficiency depends upon. It clearly depends partly on ordinary economic efficiency, which I shall henceforth call E-efficiency. Given a set of needs, projects and desires, their satisfaction will be improved by an increase in E-efficiency. S-efficiency and E-efficiency come apart because some projects and desires require more resources for their satisfaction than others. Further, some total patterns of preferences make it more expensive in terms of resources to satisfy needs. The resource cost of food in the UK, for example, is higher than in some other societies.

A project or object of desire must be *realistically available* if a person is to have the opportunity to pursue or choose it. Thus a society may be comparatively S-inefficient if the projects and objects of desire that are realistically available are more resource-expensive than in another. Also, a society may be comparatively S-inefficient if the projects and objects of desire its members *actually choose* require more resources than those of another. They may choose the more resource-costly ones either because the cheaper ones are not realistically available, or simply because they prefer them.

I now put forward a simple thesis. Market economies are essentially dynamic. Among the changes they have historically induced are the following:

(1) Meeting needs has come to require more resources as the society develops.

(2) The projects and objects of desire realistically available have come to require more resources for their pursuit and satisfaction.
(3) The projects and objects of desire actually chosen have come to require more resources for their pursuit and satisfaction.

An increase in S-inefficiency would not result from any one or two of these, if it were sufficiently offset by gains in efficiency elsewhere. It is clear, however, that such offsetting gains have not usually been enough. It is also clear that the thesis is broadly true: the dynamism of markets, as we have experienced it, has had the stated effects, and so there has been a decline in S-efficiency.

To avoid a possible misunderstanding, let me say that to say this is not at all to deny that the workings of market economies have brought net benefits to mankind. A decrease in S-efficiency is entirely compatible with an increase in well-being, and that is in fact what much of the world has experienced.

The point is also distinct from consequences of the principle of diminishing marginal utility. According to that principle, if a person is to gain the same increment in utility starting from a higher level of utility as from a lower one, more resources will generally be required. £1000 will get a young man his first usable car. He values highly the freedom to travel, and so his utility increases a lot. To make it go up as much again, far more will be needed - perhaps a Porsche or Ferrari. By contrast, my point partly concerns different resource costs for the same preferences - for example in the case of needs - and partly different resource costs between different preference schedules.

3

The main reason why market economies have evolved towards decreasing S-efficiency is, in outline, simple. The principal part of the explanation is that they have so evolved because they could. As productivity increases in the rate of transformation of raw materials, and as innovation progresses, new, resource-expensive projects and objects of desire become available. Some people will choose these, for a variety of reasons, from mere curiosity to the persuasion of salespeople. Worthwhile projects that use fewer resources become less valued, cease to be available, or at least become difficult. A decrease in S-efficiency, together with an overall increase in well-being, is in fact just what is to be expected from economic progress, at least for a time. Schumacher seemed to intend his claim that modern economies are surpassingly inefficient as a kind of paradox, since we have become so accustomed to the idea that capitalism is efficient, but once the ambiguity in 'efficient' is disclosed, the appearance of paradox evaporates.

4

There are circumstances in which we could even afford to be complacent about S-inefficiency. If the world were still sufficiently empty, so that it could absorb the effects of human activity without lasting detriment, we would not need to bother whether we were behaving in an S-efficient way. Indeed in the earlier period of industrial civilisation, S-efficiency could largely be ignored. The rate of discovery of resources, and the increased ability to exploit them given by technology, together with the fact that few people were actually using large quantities of resources, made it reasonable not to worry about S-efficiency. Growth in the conventional sense would lead to increases in general quality of life, even if S-efficiency declined. But our world is no longer like that. It is clear that, given finite resources, increases in well-being must eventually require increases in S-efficiency. There is increasing understanding that the world has reached this point. Progress must involve reversing the historical trend, so that we learn to increase well-being in ways that actually increase S-efficiency. *How* this can be done is in many respects unclear, but *that* it can in principle be done should not be in dispute. This fact can be used to defuse, in part (but only in part), a standard source of resistance to the environmentalist's message. People do not want to believe that humankind is approaching limits set by a finite world, because they fear the consequences for their well-being, seeing that cherished lifestyles would need to be abandoned.

There is nothing new about having to abandon cherished lifestyles. Only in a static world would this not have to happen, and one of the few things we can confidently believe about the future is that the world will continue to change. Whether environmentalists are right or wrong, people will live differently in the future. Those who particularly love to consume heavily have no privileged exemption. If they do have to change, they will have cause to regret having to, and so their fear is not misplaced. So this source of fear of the environmentalists' message cannot be defused.

What can be defused is the fear that the use of fewer resources *must* lower well-being. First, as Lovins and Weizsacker argue in *Factor Four*, great reductions can be made in the use of resources by more thoroughgoing application of known technologies.[6] Existing projects can be pursued much more S-efficiently, by improvement in E-efficiency. We cannot tell how far this process can be carried. But secondly, and even more importantly, we cannot tell what shape future projects will take. People may well find new worthwhile projects, or revive former ones, whose realisation takes few resources, and provides for their well-being in an S-efficient way. Civilisation is young, and people who look back at the late twentieth century in two hundred years' time may marvel at our technological primitivism.

5

The concept of S-efficiency is also of use in considering the effect of environmental policy measures. Some such measures can be considered essentially defensive. For example, prohibiting a nature reserve from being ploughed over, or turned into a business park, creates an enclave, protected against the effects of acting on values that would otherwise prevail. It is likely by itself to do little or nothing to change those values, and may simply transfer the conflict between environmental values and conventional growth to other sites. Other measures encourage or induce changes in behaviour that may in turn lead to changes in values. For example, restrictions on car parking are often imposed simply to ease traffic congestion. One does not have to subscribe to any particularly green values to find congestion undesirable. Its undesirability is a simple consequence of the fact that journeys usually have a desired destination, which congestion impedes. But the restrictions on cars may lead more people to take to bicycling, and some of them may then discover that they actually prefer to travel this way. Membership of cycling clubs may increase, and some may decide to do without their cars altogether. If such changes as these predominate, there will be a gain in S-efficiency. People will enjoy their travelling as much as or more than before, but will use fewer resources in doing so. To take another case, suppose it comes to be judged necessary, to prevent global warming, to impose much higher taxes on fossil fuels. People will not only adapt, but many of them will make a virtue out of necessity. That is, the tax was introduced because it had to be, but people come to think that their new patterns of behaviour, induced by the tax, are desirable anyway. They may thus suffer no net loss of utility, while using fewer resources.

Changes in S-efficiency can come about for less weighty reasons. Consider the fashion for making jeans out of hemp instead of cotton denim. No doubt part of the appeal of this fashion is the association of hemp with an illegal drug. It looks *cheeky* to wear hemp. But hemp is much more easily grown than cotton. It requires no pesticides and far less water. Hemp is also a tougher fibre than cotton, and so the jeans last longer. Switching from cotton to hemp yields a gain in S-efficiency. Fashion being of its nature fickle, such improvements are readily reversible, but a change that started for one reason may be continued for another.

The most important influence on S-efficiency, however, must be the attitudes of individuals towards it. If we do not care what share of the world's resources we take, we shall have a comparatively uncritical attitude towards our own projects and desires. If the pursuit of projects and desires yields the expected satisfactions, and each of us as individuals can continue to afford to continue these pursuits, we shall have no call to change. But once people begin to care, they start to discriminate among possible projects on grounds of S-efficiency, and this can have far-reaching effects. People's altruism is notoriously limited, and their sense of justice is underpowered in relation to the demands made on it. They will not, with rare exceptions, sacrifice much well-being for the sake of others. But particular ways of seeking that well-being may make them feel uncomfortable, and that may be enough to induce a search for ways of attaining well-being in more S-efficient ways. The further this search is carried, and by more people, the easier it becomes to find what one is seeking. The main reason for this is the power of the market. Once people looking for S-efficiency realise that eating locally grown vegetables is more S-efficient than eating those flown in from Africa, some farmer in their area will pick up the signals and start a vegetable box scheme. Once people start wanting tiles made from the local clay to roof their houses, quarries reopen. If you want your savings to help restore old buildings, there is a building society which will use your money specially for this purpose. If you want to invest in the development of organic farms, there is a bank with a savings account that will do just this. Such examples could be added to indefinitely. The market responses I have mentioned involve existing technology. The search for S-efficiency is also a source of innovation, such as improved photovoltaic cells.

That may sound naïve, by underestimating the power of the great corporations, and the many forms it takes, from influence on governments to the manipulation of information to form opinions convenient to the businesses themselves. It is also true that certain choices are very difficult and confusing, because the information that is readily available is inadequate or difficult to assess, or because a company seems to be doing both good and ill, so that no simple attitude is appropriate. But people's powerlessness and passivity can be exaggerated, and their resentment of power and suspicion of manipulation themselves provide some protection. Big corporations are not impervious to public opinion, and their power to form it is strongly limited by the public's awareness of that very power.

It is not part of the philosopher's task to make predictions. The aim here is merely to outline possibilities. The central claim of possibility is this: that there could be a widespread search for S-efficiency, taking the form of pursuit of ways of satisfying needs, and choices of projects and objects of desire, that could, over time, be substantially successful, so that a high quality of life was generally available with a greatly reduced throughput of resources. Such success would require a transformation of lifestyles, and the patterns of economic activity in a society so transformed would be very different from present ones.

A foreseeable objection is that the search for S-efficiency would be self-defeating. For employment is essential to a high quality of life, and with a reduced throughput and even more advanced technology, there would be a serious lack of jobs. A radical answer to this would be to say that the importance of employment is a contingent feature of certain social arrangements, but another answer is perhaps more credible. The successful pursuit of S-efficient quality of life does not entail that all projects are successfully and perfectly pursued, or all desires satisfied. People can continue indefinitely to want improvements, and be willing to call on the services of others to provide them. The point is that the process of making such improvements would not, in the circumstances envisaged, use extra resources, except for renewable ones, and especially human time. For example, a gourmet may seek more and more elaborately prepared and presented food. To meet his desires, the restaurants he patronises may need more and more chefs and waiters, but no bigger cookers. Perfection in the home may require more and more exquisite furniture, which takes no more wood to make than a country table, but a lot more human skill and time. So human insatiability takes many forms, not all of which require extra resources other than the skill and time of human beings. So, even within the unconventional framework outlined here, one may conclude that there will always be plenty of wants that people will be willing to pay to have satisfied.

6

In the quotation with which I started, Schumacher expresses another scepticism. It is clear that he does not believe that general well-being could be achieved by further growth, even if there were no environmental constraints on it. He believes that very many of us have succumbed to what I call *Vronsky's mistake*. In Tolstoy's novel, Vronsky believes that happiness consists in getting what you want. He, of course, wanted Anna Karenina. He got her, discovered his mistake, and the outcome was tragedy. If getting what you want is to contribute to happiness, you must be informed about the nature of what you want, but this is not enough. Vronsky satisfied that condition. It must also be true that having what you want must not disappoint. This is a distinct condition, because in the case of some wanted things, the information available in advance cannot be enough to tell you what it will be like to have it. Your own experience is essential, and it is not available in advance of attainment. Thus suppose I have never eaten okra, and want to eat some, after having its taste and texture described to me. I may be as fully informed in advance as I can be, but still not fully know what it will be like, and it could still disappoint me. Vronsky could not fully know in advance what it would be like to make love to Anna, but there is no suggestion that in this he was disappointed. A third condition, if satisfied desire is to contribute to happiness, is that there are no further negative consequences that outweigh the satisfaction. This is where Vronsky went wrong. It is also important to distinguish between being in error about the desired object and being in error about oneself. One may be as fully informed as possible about the object, but be disappointed because of a false belief that - to put it generally - one is the sort of person who enjoys that kind of thing. The satisfaction of desire can in this way be a form of self-discovery, and sometimes a painful one. It has mnemonic value, although it is not entirely true to the novel, to say that we have a case of Vronsky's mistake when getting what you want fails to live up to expectations on account of any kind of error.

When a person pursues a project which is in one of these ways wrong for her, a particular sort of S-inefficiency results. Success in the project will not usually be an unmitigated disaster. Characteristically, it does something towards one's well-being, but less than expected. Usually, another project, calling for no more resources, would have done more. But this is significantly different from pursuing a project which does yield all that is expected, when the pursuit of another would have yielded as much with fewer resources. I have so far concentrated on this latter case, but the former may be highly significant. There is generally a self-interested reason for avoiding S-inefficiency of the former sort. For example, suppose Jack decides to take up sailing, buys a boat, and joins a yacht club. He finds it gives him only moderate enjoyment. Suppose instead he had put the same resources into building a conservatory, and that this would have done more for his well-being. Jack had a self-interested reason to build the conservatory instead of buying the boat. But one does not always have a self-interested reason to choose a project that uses fewer resources rather than one that uses more, if both projects yield all that is expected of them. Josephine, who is interested in the Middle Ages, might be choosing between learning to read Dante in Italian and visiting all the sites of Cistercian Abbeys in France. The latter is the more resource intensive project. Suppose she can get a travel scholarship for the abbey project, and that whichever she chooses, she would find its fulfilment as wonderful as she expects, and she judges each as wonderful as the other. There is no self-interested reason for choosing the one that requires fewer resources. An ethical reason might determine Josephine's choice - though in this particular case it might seem overscrupulous in her if it were to do so.

Since self-interest is so prevalent, there is reason to emphasise cases like Jack's, but reflection on this and other examples makes us realise how much uncertainty remains ineliminable. Of course we all want to choose projects whose pursuit and attainment will contribute as much as possible to our well-being, but however hard we try to become well-informed, about ourselves, the nature of the projects, and the further consequences of pursuing it, the possibility that we shall go wrong remains a real one. Jack may have done his epistemic best before buying his boat. That he was a victim of a form of Vronsky's mistake was not at all his fault. More generally, those whose lifestyles endorse the continuing global productive project, if they are in error from the point of view of their own interests - and we should admit that frequently they are not - are not *stupidly* so. Advice to individuals to seek S-efficiency in their individual interest is redundant and unhelpful. Pointing out ethical reasons for the search may be unwelcome, but is not redundant. Most pertinent is to provide evidence that if there is to be an acceptable level of general well-being, greater S-efficiency is actually necessary.

It has long been a commonplace of environmental writing that humanity is running up against the limits of the planet, and that we must make do with less. Here I have tried to conceptualise the making do in a particular, Schumacherian way, to stress that this making do, if it is to yield well-being, involves learning and experimentation, and to claim that in this process markets can be our allies. Raising humanity S-efficiently to hitherto unknown levels of well-being is, I hope, the next great stage in the global human adventure.

Notes

1   E.F. Schumacher, 'Resources for Industry', Ch 8 of *Small is Beautiful*, London, 1993 (Vintage Books ed), pp. 95-96.

2   Herman E. Daly and John B. Cobb, Appendix to *For the Common Good*, London (Green Print), 1989. See also Tim Jackson, *Material Concerns*, London (Routledge), 1996, Ch 9 and references therein.

3   Henry David Thoreau, *Walden*, London (Everyman's Library), 1992 ed, p.7.

4   Masanobu Fukuoka, *The Natural Way of Farming*, Madras (Bookventure), 1993, p.263.

5   Aristotle, *Eudemian Ethics*, 1249b29.

6   Amory B. Lovins and Ernst von Weizsacker, *Factor Four*, London (Earthscan), 1997.

5 The Communitarian Critique of the Market

TOBY LOWE

Communitarianism is often associated with agnosticism over economic issues.[1] In this vein it is conceived as a moral critique of our cultural and political values which has little impact on the economic sphere, particularly the manner in which that sphere is structured. It is hoped that this paper will go some way to disproving this viewpoint. I hope to demonstrate that a commitment to recognising the manner in which individuals inescapably define themselves in relation to, and exist within, communities of meaning results in a powerful critique of market structures and ideology.

What is Community and Why is it Relevant to the Market?

For communitarianism to provide us with a solid base from which to criticise the market, it is first necessary to say something about the nature of the communities we are seeking to defend. The definition which will be used here is that community consists of a group of people who intersubjectively share identity-forming narratives.[2] Thus a community is an amorphous group which has certain shared self-defined stories and understandings which marks its members off from other human beings. Individuals in a community share a wider subjectivity which ties them to one another; the content and manner of that sharing being given by the narratives which are important to that community.

In this manner, community is vital to human beings. It provides both the raw materials and the tools which individuals use to forge their identities. We define ourselves in relation to those around us, and we do so using the content of the stories we share with them. Therefore, in order for us to have some measure of control over our own identities, we must address how the communal narratives, from which this identity is drawn, are formed. These communal narratives are our joint descriptions and understandings of the world in which we live. Therefore, they are strongly related to the material conditions of existence, and how these conditions are produced. For this reason we can demand an economics which respects community.

This definition of community gives us three criteria for assessing whether the economic structures and beliefs associated with free-markets are community-respecting:

- Does it respect our intersubjective links?
- Can it acknowledge a narrative-based understanding of the world?
- Is it ethical?

The first two criteria are associated with the empirical nature of our definition of community. The intersubjective criterion is a measure of how market philosophy respects the manner in which we are socially constructed in relation to our fellow community members. The narrative criterion refers to the manner in which we come to understand the world. It requires that market philosophy understand the manner in which practices and beliefs come to exist in relation to specific histories and the accounts given by the communities concerned.[3]

The final criterion represents the intrinsically normative aspect of community. This is not simply, as is often mistakenly asserted, that communities have norms which must be respected. Rather, it refers to an observation made by Raymond Plant, that debate about community 'is not about facts perceived through the senses... but rather a debate fundamentally about the kind of society in which we ought to live'.[4] Thus communities have an inescapably ethical component because they are constantly considering how people should relate to one another. The ethical criterion serves as a measure of the extent to which market ideology and practices allow or encourage this sort of reflection and examination to occur. In this way, we can also see that the three criteria are not entirely separate. The first two criteria cannot be free from normative considerations because they help to define a term which itself has inescapably normative dimensions.

We now turn to the task of examining how market philosophy matches up to the criteria which have been established.

Market-Intersubjectivity Assessed

The first argument we have to consider is that free-market capitalism is based on a model of economic rationality which utilises human interdependency in the most efficient manner possible. Thus, the claim is that whilst economic rationality leads individuals to make decisions along self-interested lines, this results in a social system in which all our needs can be met. However, in this section we will question the manner in which market relations encourage us to focus on our relationships with others in an instrumental fashion. We will question whether this focus on meeting needs of others to satisfy our own individual interests is compatible with a social definition of selfhood.

Firstly, the idea that what we produce, and whom we should distribute it to, should be a function solely of *personal* self-interest, seems to violate the idea that production should recognise the intersubjectivity of selfhood. If our economic calculations are based solely on what is good for us, where does this leave our relationships with others?

At this point it might occur to us to ask why a claim about the nature of our subjectivity should affect our evaluation of particular types of economic relationship. Are we violating the infamous fact/value divide?

The reply to this is that it is perfectly possible to bridge the fact/value gap because the model of subjectivity which is used for social explanation strongly affects how individuals relate to one another. If individual subjectivity is built around a model of autonomous individuals, then the model of mutual obligation which is constructed around those subjects will struggle to accommodate a view which suggests that the quality and content of their relationships, their interdependence, is an important factor in assessing their moral responsibilities. In other words, a moral theory based around autonomous individuals will likely place all moral responsibilities upon individual agents, and find notions of collective responsibility difficult to theorise. This can be clearly seen in Nozick's theory of moral responsibility which falls solely on individuals and not social systems.[5] This means that there is no reason for individuals to feel responsible for the manner in which their beliefs and behaviour contribute to generating a social context for others, because those other individuals are entirely responsible for their own behaviour, irrespective of context.

However, if individual subjectivity is conceived intersubjectively, as we have described, then the scenario is very different. Under this model we can be held responsible for the manner in which we affect others through our contribution to their social context, because, in an important sense, we are an integral part of their identity.

We can see, therefore, how different explanations of the nature of our subjectivity can result in different moral evaluations. Under the terms which we have developed a failure to recognise the intersubjective nature of identity will result in a derogation of our moral responsibilities because it will cause us to conceive those responsibilities in a very limited fashion. This is why the intersubjective criterion is vital.

The capitalist candidature for the intersubjective criterion is that whilst there is no immediate concern for others, everyone is looking out for themselves so that, overall, the whole community is catered for. However, this fails to acknowledge that the quality of relationships is ignored in such a system. The idea that the motivation for production is to satisfy our own needs encourages us to take an instrumental view of others. Thus, as Adam Smith pointed out, we cannot expect the baker to give us bread simply because we need it, we can only expect it if we can meet one of his needs.[6] Thus, if we are unable to pay for the goods we desire, our needs go unmet. My suffering may be painful to the baker, since, as human beings, we have the intersubjective link which allows us to share each other's pain, but this cannot be recognised, since, on this instrumental view, I will only help you if you help me.

This is by no means a fatal point against the market system, since there is no reason why a community should not be founded on reciprocity - after all this would seem to represent an ideal way of ensuring that the interdependencies generated by intersubjectivity do not become one-way *dependencies* of one person on another. If I want help from the baker in meeting my need for bread, I shouldn't expect something for nothing, I should trade something for a loaf, or offer my services to the baker for a period of time. Further, as Acton argued, if the baker was successful, and had loaves to spare, there is no reason why he could not meet my needs through a charitable act. Therefore, it seems that, at this level, free-market capitalism is perfectly capable of acknowledging our intersubjective links.

However, if we look deeper, we can find flaws with this argument. The instrumentality of economic self-interest is more important than we have so far acknowledged, especially when we flesh out our theoretical bakery with a little realism. The bakery is now located within a large supermarket. Now it is no longer possible for me to 'help' the baker in return for a loaf in any other way than with monetary payment. I cannot barter anything I may have produced, I cannot offer to help behind the counter for a day. I need access to means of producing wealth, either directly, or through employment for wages. If for any reason (and there are any number of good reasons why I might not have access in these ways - for example disability, or long-term structural unemployment) I cannot get access to income, then my needs are simply ignored. Here, the instrumentality of market relationships is felt in full force and individual self-interest negates the link between my need and the person who is capable of meeting it.

Neither is it enough to suggest that charitable instincts in people will ensure that my needs are met. There are a number of reasons for this. Firstly, charitable giving is unpredictable, and therefore cannot be relied upon to meet basic needs such as food. Secondly, charitable giving depends upon sympathy from one party to another. This sympathy can be lessened by market sustaining narratives: economic self-interest - that we should all stand on our own two feet - can easily lead to accusations of 'scrounging'. Moreover, the identification with the plight of another, which is central to the motivation to charity, can be lessened by the fragmentation associated with market societies. We will explore this argument in more detail in the critique of market narratives.

It would seem then that focusing on individual economic interest does violate those responsibilities to others which stem from the social nature of human existence, because it privileges desires which can be paid for above needs which, for whatever reason, cannot. The capitalist reply to this, as we can see from Hayek and Acton,[7] is to assert that benevolence is all very well as a productive criterion in a small tribal unit, but that the 'extended order' of our modern industrial societies means that we cannot know what others require. Thus each must assert their own needs through market relations, otherwise the freedom from chronic poverty which industrial society has granted us will be lost in wasted production and inefficient distribution. The key notion is therefore that the efficiency gained by basing transactions on self-interest justifies any temporary problems people may experience with the system. Hayek states,

> The point is not that whatever economists determine to be efficient is therefore 'right', but that economic analysis can elucidate the usefulness of practices heretofore thought to be right - usefulness from the perspective of any philosophy that looks unfavourably on the human suffering and death that could follow from the collapse of our civilisation.[8]

The argument is now, therefore, that although economic self-interest results in production for profit, rather than for meeting needs directly, and therefore can produce individual instances which appear not to be 'right', the overall wealth-generating capacity of the capitalist mode of production justifies its existence.

Now, the first thing that we can notice about this argument is that it appears to contradict the standard market argument that it is individual transactions which can be judged as just or unjust, and not the overall state of affairs.[9] Thus two lines of attack are opened up. Firstly, that this new concern with the overall level of production masks individual injustices, such as certain people's basic needs not being met. This strengthens our critique of the instrumentality of market relationships, allowing us to suggest that the market system ignores the quality of our social relationships, submerging it in a concern for the overall level of production. Secondly, if justification of the economic system is now to be allowed on the overall results it produces, then we can criticise the overall shape of the distribution that results. This line of argument will be pursued later, when commenting on the ethics of market distribution.

We are now in a position to examine whether the criterion which Hayek is using to justify the capitalist economic system - a level and diversity of production sufficient to meet overall human need - is as forceful an argument as he thinks. The standard argument against this idea comes from J. K. Galbraith, who asserts that since production has been divorced from immediate need - we are producing for exchange and not use - production becomes an end in itself rather than a means to fulfilling human wants or needs.[10] The next stage in the argument is to point out that since we produce for production's sake, rather than for need, the desires for the products that we produce must be *created by advertising*.[11]

The overall thrust of this argument is therefore that the goal of increased production does not satisfy the social needs of any community, but rather is necessary simply because our incomes rely on a system which requires ever increasing growth to survive. Thus the capitalist system is not simply recognising and serving the needs of interdependent individuals, rather it is forcing us to adopt a materialist, consumption-oriented mentality in order to absorb the ever-increasing level of production. Thus the attack on the quality of our social relationships comes in two ways. Firstly, the emphasis on ever increasing production in a competitive environment encourages the subordination of the needs of employees, as will be discussed in the next section. Secondly, the emphasis on individuals as consumers tends to promote an atomising culture in which the consumption of private goods takes priority over our social relations.

There are problems with this critique.[12] However, this is not the end of the matter, as we can make two further arguments against Hayek. Firstly, Galbraith's critique can be refined to suggest that the problem lies with the fact that we do not have any social control mechanisms over what is produced and how. This means that the brute fact of production cannot be made to serve any other master, such as social or environmental needs. This argument will be explored in full in a later section, but for the moment, we will have to be content with the idea that Hayek's argument that the capitalist productive system is justified because it supports human needs is, at the least, contestable.

Secondly, the notion of efficiency resulting from the profit motive can be challenged in terms of the quality of relationships which it can sustain. Profit maximisation on the part of employers, combined with global competition, has led to an increased demand for 'flexible' labour. It is the new clarion-call of politicians and businessmen - labour must be flexible if firms are to compete in global markets. This means that employees must, as standard, be prepared to work anti-social hours, they must be prepared to swap shifts weekly, they must not expect job security, and they must expect wage settlements in line with their global competitors.

Here we can clearly see that the obsession with producing at the lowest possible unit cost is not compatible with an outlook which is concerned with the web of social relationships in which individuals exist. Flexible employment is a nightmare for personal relationships, in that variable shifts can easily leave partners with no waking time to spend together or with their children. Socialising with friends becomes difficult as working anti-social hours lessens the possibility of reaffirming our social bonds of friendship through the normal social activities of sharing meals, going out together at the week-ends - simply spending time in each other's company.

Further, the job insecurity associated with flexible labour destroys potential co-operative relationships between co-workers, and especially between those employed by competing firms. The fact of insecurity is known to workers, who know they must then compete against their colleagues in order that when 'downsizing' occurs, it will not be they who are sacked. This results in lessened co-operation between co-workers, destroying potential solidarities by using the principle of divide and rule. This process is even more extreme between firms (or regions, or states - any competing economic actors) which are engaged competitively. Restrictions on trade union activity in the 1980s, especially relating to secondary picketing, mean that rather than being able to support workers in different sectors in their discussions over wages and conditions, employees of one firm, or workers in one region etc., now experience a lowering of wages, or a lessening of restrictions on working conditions, as competition for production or, in the case of regions or states, 'inward investment'. Thus rather than being able to form solidarities with workers in similar positions, employees are related by links of mutual suspicion and fear as they 'bid down' both wages and working conditions.

We have seen, then, that free market relationships do not represent a plausible interpretation of the social nature of individual existence. The instrumental nature of market relationships violates the communal nature of individual identity, by encouraging us to treat others as if they were entirely alien. Further, this cannot be justified by an appeal to the overall level of need or want satisfaction in society, as the manner in which production and consumption occurs has further atomising and anti-social results.

Market-Narratives Assessed

Now we will turn to the second criterion, the free-market interpretation of the narrative nature of human action. Hayek asserts that free-market relationships are the product of allowing narratives to evolve freely. This is driven by a process of cultural evolution motivated by the human desire to make life comfortable and secure.

The idea, therefore, is that the narrative traditions which we have developed to deal with property and trade represent the wisdom of thousands of years of accumulated practice of individuals creating solutions to their particular problems. Free-market capitalism with its institutions of private property and free-trade are thus natural, spontaneous organisational systems. He opposes this to the socialist belief that society can be 'designed' in accordance with human reason in order to serve some particular goal. Thus he states,

> One's initial surprise at finding that intelligent people tend to be socialists diminishes when one realises that, of course, intelligent people will tend to overvalue intelligence, and to suppose that one must owe all the advantages and opportunities that our civilisation offers to deliberate design rather than to following traditional rules, and likewise to suppose that we can, by exercising our reason, eliminate any remaining undesired features by still more rational reflection, and still more appropriate design and 'rational co-ordination' of our understandings.[13]

Does this satisfy our criterion that an economic system acknowledge the narrative nature of human action? The answer to this question is a definite 'no', since it relies on an impoverished view of what narratives are and their relationship to human reason and agency.

70

Hayek's argument depends on the view that market narratives are spontaneously generated, and any other views are a product of 'interference' with market mechanisms in the name of spurious reasoning. We can examine this view and find it severely deficient.

Firstly, market narratives do not represent any spontaneous or natural ordering of human behaviour. If this was the case then some version of free-market trading would represent the norm for all human cultures, which it clearly does not. To many traditional cultures, such as aboriginal cultures in Australia, or Inuit cultures in North America, the structures and practices of the market are completely alien, and have been imposed on them through government 'interference'. Edward Gondolf, writing about the experience of the introduction of capitalism into traditional Alaskan communities, states,

> The organisational structure was not suited to the native experience: it divided the previously united Natives into local groups, thus diminishing their political clout... The corporations brought a cash economy to an otherwise subsistence life-style. Traditional patterns of leadership were usurped by the corporate structure, and family relations based on kinship and subsistence sharing were sorely taxed... According to the Hydaburg residents, [one of the communities where the study took place] a loss of self-worth and identity accompanies corporate resource development and is manifest in an extreme amount of alcoholism and drug abuse, rated as the top problem of the town.[14]

In this particular case, therefore, market narratives were imposed by direct government legislation. Is there any reason to suppose that markets evolved spontaneously and without government 'interference' in all other cultures? The answer would seem to be given by market theorists who admit that authority has played a significant role in gaining market narratives their dominant cultural position. Hayek states,

> Governments strong enough to protect individuals against the violence of their fellows *make possible* the evolution of an increasingly complex order of spontaneous and voluntary co-operation.[15] (my emphasis)

This is an important acknowledgement for market theorists to make since we can see how market narratives have become the dominant economic paradigm *because* they have had the support of powerful business interests who stand to gain most from their general acceptance. We can provide concrete examples of exactly the sort of behaviour. The manner in which capitalism has been imposed on countries against the express wishes of their inhabitants through covert military action, often by the United States, seems to indicate that free-market narratives are anything but spontaneous.[16]

Thus a plausible argument exists that the neo-liberal, free-market doctrines are just as much a product of 'interference' and 'rational design' as any socialist's view. Is there any way of judging whether this argument is correct, or whether Hayek's view of the natural evolutionary nature of market narratives remains intact?

If we examine the method by which Hayek comes to his conclusion, then it would seem possible to rule conclusively in favour of the argument that market narratives are as constructed as any other. What we find is that Hayek reaches his conclusion only by arbitrarily privileging the science of economics over all other disciplines. Thus Hayek states sociology is a spurious discipline because it 'proceeds in sovereign disregard of knowledge gained by established disciplines that have long studied such grown structures as law, language and the market.'[17] He also criticises Jacques Monod for basing his arguments in a theory of knowledge which 'has attempted to develop a science of behaviour whether called eudaemonism, utilitarianism, socialism, or whatever - on the grounds that certain sorts of behaviour better satisfy our wishes.'[18]

This wildly dismissive statement might be acceptable if we placed it in Hayek's general argument against what he calls 'scientism', the idea that we can rationally remake the world according to abstract scientific principles. However, it appears that certain social sciences, namely economics, manage to escape the evils of scientism. He states that scientism 'leads intellectuals to disregard a world of scientific and historical information, to remain ignorant of the biological sciences, and *the sciences of man such as economics*.'[19] (my emphasis)

It is implausible for Hayek to attempt to draw a legitimate distinction between economics as an acceptable social science, and others which attempt to develop a science of behaviour. From what we have seen of Hayek's method, it is clear that he begins with the assumption he is trying to prove, that economic self-interest, leading to capitalist relations, is natural for human beings. This is why disciplines which 'proceed in sovereign disregard of... the market', such as sociology, are automatically spurious.

This assumption leads Hayek to see any challenges to market narratives as being the product of government intervention, rather than being another narrative which is challenging for dominance. For instance, he assumes that there has been a steady and spontaneous evolution of human narratives towards a free market situation. However, this leads him to completely disregard rival historical studies, such as those of Karl Polanyi. Block and Somers, summarising Polanyi's thought, suggest that,

> The road to the free market was paved with continuous political manipulation, whether the state was actively involved in removing old restrictive regulations, as in the case of Spain, or building new political administrative bodies to bolster the factors of production of the new market economy, as in the administrative mechanisms of the New Poor Law.[20]

Polanyi further challenges the notion of a natural market narrative by documenting the existence of what he calls a 'double-movement'. That is, any evolutionary changes in market structures automatically produce their own response from that section of society which is affected by them. Thus the formation of trade unions, or the fight against the enclosure movement in England, were not driven by an ideological scientism, but evolved as counter-narrative responses to changes in people's material circumstances.[21]

Thus we can see that it is more appropriate to view all narratives, and not just market ones, as constructed by people in response to their material conditions mediated through the beliefs which sustain their particular community. These competing narratives can gain a dominant position through co-opting the authority of government power. This applies as much to neo-liberal market doctrines as it does to 'socialist' responses to them. Only by adopting the blinkered view that market narratives are the only natural and spontaneously generated means to sustain society can Hayek maintain that his narrative view is plausible. Once these assumptions are stripped away, Hayek's position becomes untenable.

However, it would be a mistake to see the failure of Hayek's quasi-historical narrative approach as the end of the discussion about capitalism's consideration of the narrative-bound nature of human action. Whilst Hayek is the only thinker who explicitly defends free markets in terms of the way in which they are generated by the *free evolution* of tradition, this idea, or ideas related to it, are implicit in all free-market thought.

We can see that this is the case in free-market ideas about the role of government and the notion of 'interference' with markets. The argument is that whilst markets need moral and legal protection from government (or some similar authority) in order to function, this does not represent government 'interference' in society, rather it prevents interference with the market mechanism, which is assumed to be natural. A distinction is drawn between governments protecting a framework for exchanges to take place, and actually being part of particular exchanges themselves. This represents a fall-back position which attempts to make Hayek's thought more tenable. Speaking about the function of government in distributive justice, Acton notes,

> Individuals exchange goods between one another; it is they who determine who gets what, not some authority over them. Government is needed, of course, to prevent violence and fraud, but the government is not party to the exchanges.[22]

Thus Acton is arguing that government power is involved in securing free-market narratives, but only after the fact, so to speak. Thus it helps to secure those narratives that exist rather than designing new ones. Government is merely helping to achieve the narratives that people already want.

However, this argument is also untenable. It ignores the manner in which individual narratives concerning economic relations are formed within an existing economic framework. Therefore, individuals within a capitalist system *do* form their economic narratives around capitalism, precisely because these are the ones protected and institutionalised by government, and hence form the dominant public narrative. This represents a failure by Acton to come to terms with the narrative view of individual behaviour, and comes down, once more, to an argument that capitalist narratives are those naturally desired by human beings, which is plainly false.

Nozick, too, makes similar assumptions about the nature of a social system based on market transactions. Governments are there in order to protect the rights of individuals and associations, and nothing else. Given that these rights are almost exclusively connected with private property and freedom in the economic realm, this results in 'a realisation of the economists' model of a competitive market'.[23] This, Nozick asserts, is the government being 'neutral between its citizens'.[24]

Thus the whole thrust of the argument is based in the idea that certain types of human behaviour - market transactions - have some quality which demands that they be institutionalised and defended by the state, and that this quality is absent from other forms of human interaction. Therefore, market narratives - the private production, exchange and consumption of goods - and the institutions and practices which they describe and sustain are viewed either as being the only natural ones, or in some way privileged over rival organisational possibilities.

We can now turn to the reasons why free market theorists have a pauperised notion of narratives. It is because they assume the validity of what

Nozick calls 'methodological individualism'. This method of philosophical reflection proposes that individuals are essentially undetermined by any social influences.[25] At first glance, this seems like a curious argument to make in respect of Nozick, because he explicitly denies the value of methodological individualism. He refers to the 'invisible hand' as a social 'filtering' process which explains patterns of social behaviour by reference to a social process which filters out results which do not fit into the market pattern.[26]

We might accept this notion of a filtering process as a simplistic version of narrative theory in that it might allow Nozick to understand why public capitalist narratives result in individual capitalist narratives by filtering out alternatives. Therefore we might think that if we find something about these narratives to be unappealing, we can look at this filtering process as a *cause*.

However, Nozick's concept of the invisible hand as a filtering process does not allow this sort of analysis. He allows no examination of causes in respect of the filtering process because of the manner in which it is described as being an 'invisible hand'. Thus he states,

> An invisible hand explanation explains what looks to be the product of someone's intentional design, as not being brought about by anyone's intentions. We might call the opposite sort of explanation a 'hidden-hand explanation'. A hidden-hand explanation explains what looks to be merely a disconnected set of facts that (certainly) is not the product of intentional design, as the product of an individual or group's intentional design(s). Some persons also find such explanations satisfying, as is evidenced by the popularity of conspiracy theories.[27]

Thus, even, though he explicitly rejects methodological individualism, he ends up bringing it back in via the back door. Although he recognises the existence of social patterns which are not the product of any individual's decision, he allows no examination of those patterns for causal powers, and therefore the only place which is left to search for causal responsibility is in the decisions of individuals.

As a consequence of the use of such individualistic narratives, the abstracted individual has no point of reference except his or her own undefined self-interest. With this as a starting point for judging the nature of human interaction, relationships naturally become conceived in individualistic instrumental terms. Economic interactions begin with discrete individuals working out what they will gain out of any transaction. It is for this reason that Hayek privileges market narratives in his historical view. If human

75

behaviour is judged in terms of the interaction of self-interested, socially undetermined individuals, then market narratives become the most plausible mode of action.

Two related failures result from this methodological individualism, in terms of a narrative view. Firstly, the way in which individuals are theorised does not recognise the way in which the choices they make are shaped by the narratives they are already using. This means that methodological individualism undermines narratives as an explanatory tool. The presentation of human action as a series of undetermined choices does not accord with the narrative view, which suggests that the collective stories we tell about how interactions work create the conditions under which future choices are made. Thus future choices are made in compliance with a particular worldview. These choices then remake the world, for which new stories are needed. But the new stories, and the choices which come from them, are all dependent on the initial stories and the choices that were made in that context. This means that theorists such as Nozick cannot arrive at a narrative understanding, and leads others such as Hayek, who attempt some form of justification in terms of a historical evolutionary process, to be blind to the fact that the idea of acting out of a certain view of 'rational self-interest' is itself a constructed narrative.

Secondly, methodological individualism undermines a narrative view because it leaves individuals unable to recognise how they are joined by narratives and are consequently unable to reflect collectively on how they are affected by them. This undermines the use of narratives as an ethical tool. This is true of Hayek's narrative individualism, as well as for the purer form espoused by Nozick.

The effect we are concerned with here is the way that concentrating on the individual sabotages our ability to see 'the big picture'. This is linked with the free-market idea that it is impossible to specify any overall just pattern or particular distribution of resources which would be just or ethical for a society. It is only possible, we remember, to judge whether individual transactions are equitable or not.

Why should this be the case? The free-market individualist case stems from seeing society as a collection of discrete individuals, each with their own set of individual ends which can never be fully comprehended by any other person. Each individual then acts on these ends, intending only his or her own benefit. These actions may have consequences for others which were not intended or foreseen, but the individual cannot take these consequences into account when assessing the morality of his or her choices since they are, from

76

the individual's perspective, unforeseeable. We can see these ideas very clearly in the work of both Hayek and Nozick. Hayek argues:

> Understandable aversion to such morally blind results, results inseparable from any process of trial-and-error, lead men to want to achieve a contradiction in terms: namely to wrest control of evolution - i.e. of the procedure of trial-and-error - and to shape it to their present wishes. But intended moralities resulting from this reaction give rise to irreconcilable claims that no system can satisfy and which thus remain the source of unceasing conflict. The fruitless attempt to render a situation just whose outcome, by its nature cannot be determined by what anyone does or can know, only damages the functioning of the process itself.[28]

Nozick phrases this in terms of the absence of a social entity:

> There is no social entity with a good that undergoes some sacrifice for its own good. There are only individual people, different individual people, with their own individual lives. Using one of these people for the benefit of others uses him and benefits the others. Nothing more. What happens is that something is done to him for the sake of others. Talk of an overall social good covers this up.[29]

Thus the picture emerges that individuals cannot judge justice or morality in the economic system as a whole because they have only their partial fragmented knowledge to go on. They cannot know or understand the effect of their actions on others. Since individuals have these discrete and separate goals, no society-wide set of goals can be specified, and therefore individuals' actions cannot be held up to such a yardstick for inspection.

However, this argument rests on the assumptions of methodological individualism. It is only by sticking rigidly to the assumptions of heavily differentiated and alienated individuals that such a pauperised view of ethics can emerge. The reason that individuals do not know the consequences of their actions is that they do not have to face up to them. By assuming that individuals are not socially determined, people can escape responsibility for creating the social conditions which form the context for other people's choices. Individuals are isolated from the products of their actions because they are not encouraged to examine how their actions are linked to the actions of other people, except in terms of self-interested instrumentalism. This is manifested when Hayek denigrates sociology and praises economics.

Thus individuals are prevented from ever coming to a realisation that any alternative is possible because the narrative presented to them is that they are all separate isolated beings, solely responsible for their own welfare. The idea that 'there is no such thing as society' becomes a self-fulfilling prophecy. Social problems do appear opaque and insoluble to isolated individuals, since their possible actions could affect the overall picture in only the most negligible fashion. Using the narrative of isolated, partial individuals as a social model creates the reality in which we become isolated, partial individuals. Therefore, we find that we must behave as the model predicts we ought to precisely because we live in the sort of world where that behaviour is most rational.

However, if these isolated individuals were to establish forums to communicate their problems to one another, discover the effect of their actions upon one another, acknowledge their links and commonalities, and devise strategies for collective action, then the situation would appear very different. Suddenly individuals are no longer at the mercy of huge impersonal forces which they cannot possibly hope to comprehend. Communicating, and learning about one another's lives, individuals do indeed discover that each is unique, but that they share many interests and needs which can best be achieved through collaboration. They are now in a position to regulate and control these social forces along lines that they themselves devise.

Thus it is possible to conclude that free-market thought comprehensively fails to meet the narrative criterion. The privileging of free-market narratives rests on the bogus assumptions of methodological individualism, which undermines the possibility of people understanding how their lives are shaped by social conditions, and therefore prevents reflection on generating new narratives which could allow them to gain control over these conditions collectively. This has extremely adverse consequences on capitalism's claim that it is ethically sensitive, as we shall discover presently.

Further, by ignoring the manner in which a community's narratives can become fragmented, free-market theorists fail to acknowledge the manner in which communities are constructed from intertwined narratives. This means that fragmented narratives result in fragmented communities. The interpretation of our narrative criterion which free-market capitalism gives, therefore, is unacceptable.

Market Ethics Assessed

We can now turn to the idea of morality in a free marketplace. Two arguments are made which attempt to suggest that free markets are not amoral: firstly that even if market transactions appear to display a lack of concern for others, morality still exists in wider society, and market transactions provide the resources for moral use.[30] Secondly, markets do display certain moral virtues such as honesty and integrity, and can accommodate other values if people so desire.[31]

The first argument concerns the separation of life into distinct realms. It is important to note that the argument is not that it is impossible for an individual to demarcate separate spheres in his or her own existence (although our capacity to do this is often overstated). Rather, the point to be made is that the separation of realms is implausible because what for one person is a purely economic matter, for another is one of extreme moral concern. Further, the issue is strongly related to the ability to control the narratives which your identity is concerned with. Thus, if a businessman manages to demarcate his own life successfully, acting out one set of characteristics during his business life, and using others at home, this will not succeed in disentangling economic concerns from moral ones overall. The people who are on the receiving end of his business directions, on matters such as wage levels, hours, and working conditions, have no ability to separate the economic from other realms because they have no ability to control the conditions and narratives which dominate their lives.

This can be seen very clearly in the case of the oil company Shell. Shell Petroleum Development Company (SPDC) is involved with a dispute with the Ogoni people, represented by the Movement for the Survival of the Ogoni People (MOSOP), whose land they are exploiting for the oil reserves it contains. MOSOP has highlighted the extreme environmental degradation carried out by Shell, the lack of respect for Ogoni land use, the lack of compensation the Ogonis have received, and the manner in which Shell has abstained from preventing its partner in this venture, the Nigerian government, from committing atrocities such as the illegal imprisonment and murder of Ogonis who protest about Shell's involvement in their region.

However, as far as Shell are concerned, their activities in Nigeria are, for them, strictly a business matter and not a moral concern. This is shown by the pamphlet issued by Shell after its activities were exposed on British television. It reads:

> SPDC believes that most of MOSOP's demands are outside the business scope of oil operating companies and within the government's sphere of responsibility. Their campaign is overtly 'political' and 'Shell' is being

unfairly used to raise the international profile of that campaign through disruption of oil operations, and environmental accusations.[32]

Thus Shell's position is that it is concerned solely with economic affairs. It is seeking to claim that there is a separation of realms between economic and moral/justice concerns, and that it is only operating within the former. From this we can see how the separation of realms argument is at best untenable, and at worst a deliberate act of hypocrisy designed to camouflage the harm done by specific economic activities. The importance of this point means that it is worth exploring this example in some detail.

The moral concerns of the Ogoni relating to environmental degradation, land use, and an appropriate share of the income generated from oil reserves discovered on their land, spring directly from Shell's economic activities. It is churlish of Shell to claim that they have no responsibility, and that the matter lies in the hands of the Nigerian government. Shell are perfectly aware that the Nigerian government is not democratic, and that the Ogoni people have no chance of having their case heard by the state.

Further, there is a strong argument to suggest that the position taken by the Nigerian state is directly connected to serving the interests of foreign petroleum producers such as Shell. Cyril Obi, in his study of Ogoni resistance, makes this case very clear, pointing out that the actions of the Nigerian government, including internal repression and the suppression of 'dissidents', have been instigated solely to keep Shell happy.[33] Evidence in support of this argument comes from documents from the Nigerian government. A memorandum entitled 'Law and Order in Ogoni etc.' from the 12 May 1994, states, 'Shell operations impossible unless ruthless military operations are undertaken for smooth economic activities to commence.'[34] It further implies that Shell paid for these operations to take place, stating that the government required, 'pressure on oil companies for prompt regular inputs, as discussed... an initial disbursement of 50 million naira as advanced allowances to officers and men, and for logistics to commence operations with immediate effect, as agreed.'[35]

Therefore, we can safely conclude that the argument surrounding the separation of an economic from a moral realm is spurious because the process of separation attempts to create an economic sphere which is exempt from ethical evaluation. The purpose behind the creation of this sphere is to attempt to mask the moral harm which can result from economic activity. The normal functioning of modern businesses[36] generates moral questions, and therefore companies must accept that they have duties which go far beyond maximising the profits of their shareholders. From an ethical perspective, it is not enough to claim that people engaged in these activities may behave morally in other areas of their life. What must be accounted for is why they should be allowed to cause harm in their economic activities.

Now that we have shown that the idea of separate moral and economic realms is bogus, it places even more importance on the second free-market argument, that markets do display moral characteristics, and are perfectly capable of expressing moral concerns and taking moral decisions. For unless capitalism can demonstrate that moral action is part of the economic sphere, it is condemned to be amoral.

This argument can be split into two parts. Firstly, that markets display their own virtues, and secondly, that markets are capable of sustaining any moral choices that people care to take.

Thus Acton contends that the market displays virtues such as honesty and reliability, even though it has trouble with other virtues such as humility and self-sacrifice.[37] The key idea here is that markets encourage the formation of a moral vision where each strives to attain their own ends, but within a framework which allows others to do the same. It is claimed that this is a moral vision which is capable of sustaining our society. Hayek describes his version as an evolved morality of saving, private property, and honesty.[38]

Thus the market displays the moral characteristics which are appropriate to sustaining a civilisation based on the extended order of a free-market society. Is this a plausible interpretation of an ethical society? Hayek asserts that it is the only plausible interpretation.[39] Is this the case?

As an interpretation of an ethical society, this vision is inadequate. It may not be a society where there is malice toward others, since one must deal honestly and fairly with those we have relationships with. However, there is no positive duty of care toward others, nor any ethic of fraternity or fellow-feeling in our dealings. The watchword in such a society is still 'caveat emptor' - buyer beware.

Are we ready to conclude, therefore, that a free-market society does not offer a plausible interpretation of our ethical criteria? Not yet, for we have one more objection to cover. This is Nozick's idea that the freedom of action granted by a system based on enlightened self-interest allows any moral values to be sustained, providing that people are prepared to adhere to them voluntarily. Market structures and attitudes do not rule any form of moral behaviour inadmissible, and therefore represent a neutral mediator of ethical decisions. He states,

Within the market, we can serve those of our fellows' desires whose serving also [morally] improves them. But the market mechanism does not especially reward us for satisfying those desires, rather than other desires that are neutral toward or even retard those people's development.

This is not a criticism of the market that our fellows can make; the market serves them no worse than they choose to be served.[40]

Thus under the market system we get what we ask for. If we seek moral ends, we can use the market to attain them, hence Nozick's belief that worker-control can exist under a free-market system, if people are willing to support it.[41] However, if we make choices that do not morally improve us, then that is nobody's fault but our own.

We can find empirical support for this position. The existence under a market system of institutions such as the Co-operative Bank, and other ethical investment trusts demonstrates that people can make and implement moral choices through the market. Further evidence is provided through the existence of ethical products such as free-range eggs, cruelty-free cosmetics or 'fair-trade' commodities such as coffee.

This seems to be a powerful argument. The market system may not be intrinsically ethical, but it allows people the freedom to express ethical choices if they so desire. Ethical decisions are thus not forced upon anyone, which itself represents an ethical stance, but can nevertheless be implemented if people so wish.

What can be done to meet this challenge? It would require an argument which claimed that there was something intrinsic to the functioning of markets which resulted in ethical decisions not being made, or at least the likelihood of their occurrence being reduced. It is therefore necessary to claim that markets undermine our ability to make and implement moral choices. In fact this is exactly the sort of argument we can make.

The key to this argument is to be found in the structural consequences of market operations and the narratives required to sustain them. Discussion of moral issues requires that the participants share enough common narratives to render their discussion meaningful to one another. The social fragmentation which results from the operation of free-markets undermines the conditions which allow the creation of common narratives to occur. Firstly, the social stratification resulting from huge inequalities of income and property means that different groups of people find it virtually impossible to communicate, as they rarely encounter one another. The rich businesswoman who lives in a recently redeveloped and gentrified quayside flat, guarded by private security firms, and surrounded by others who can afford this sort of service, simply never encounters and engages with the life of a single-mother on a council housing estate who struggles to bring up her children amidst an environment of poverty and crime.

Ethical action depends on these two people coming together and negotiating the terms of their interaction. Without this debate, there is no way to know whether one is behaving ethically toward another, since the partial knowledge that each of the actors possesses is not enough to base any judgement upon. This simply does not occur under highly stratified conditions. Geographical separation occurs because those who can afford decent housing separate themselves from 'problem' estates. Social separation occurs because our leisure facilities are also income-dependent. The rich businesswoman drinks in expensive bars which provide exclusivity and social status, the single mother, if she goes out at all, attends local social clubs where there are no travel expenses, and the costs are low.

This situation results in the idea of different moral universes. These people's lives are so estranged that it is virtually impossible for them to find common narratives which they can use to begin to understand how their relationships could be ethically based. The lack of any understanding of the other's situation means that they have no choice but to treat the other instrumentally, and act in a self-interested manner. The other person's life is so alien to them, how can they begin to form a bond of commonality with them?

Thus we can argue that free-markets violate the conditions necessary to generate ethical action. The free-market response that we cannot morally judge the overall distribution in society is bogus, as we have seen. Justification was given for the free market system (even though it was not described as justification) on the grounds that it sustained society through its overall ability to make efficient use of resources. Therefore, if we can demonstrate that the overall resource allocation fails to sustain society in certain respects, namely the vital ability to generate ethical debate, then this is a valid criticism within free-market theorists' own terms.

Further, as we saw in the evaluation of market narratives, the idea that we cannot judge the overall social picture is a function of the way in which individuals are kept isolated from one another. The narrative which sustains market institutions and allows people to function within them, encourages people to see themselves as autonomous, self-serving figures, who do not directly care about the welfare of others. We can now see this for what it is - an attempt to legitimate the socially stratified system. Market conditions create a situation where people cannot comprehend the lives and goals of others, leaving them with no choice but to act on their own self-interest. Therefore, narratives arise to explain and socially reify this situation. These narratives then encourage further self-interested decisions, which keeps society locked into a vicious circle of alienation.

Is this relying on too deterministic a description of human behaviour? What about people's ability to reflect on their actions? The response to this is that people are reflecting on their actions within this situation, but the nature of the information readily available to them, and the way that this information is processed through existing narratives, means that escape from the circle is made more unlikely. The form of reflection and debate which might allow people to escape is effectively denied precisely because the full range of opinions is never heard; certain people's stories are hidden because they have no voice in a system based around the idea of self-interested production and consumption.

While people may have access to reflection, and therefore, from their perspective, ethical action, it will be at best a partial reflection. Thus it is plausible to suggest that the market is not a neutral system for taking and implementing ethical decisions, rather it is a very poor and inefficient transmission mechanism. There is no escape from 'the bottom line' that economic transactions under a free-market capitalist system are conducted on the basis of self-interest - the profit motive. Therefore, as Acton states, 'What should be emphasised is that whatever their non-market aims, motives and ideals, they [businessmen] will not promote them by buying too dear or selling too cheap in market terms.'[42]

The profit motive renders ethical concerns subordinate, secondary considerations. The idea is that business must be conducted on the basis of narrow 'economic' criteria, which may then be regulated by ethical considerations. This is an impoverished way to include ethics in economic transactions because it establishes the goal of production prior to ethical considerations. It is based on the individualistic model of moral decision making:

Individual Interest
vs.   =   Outcome
Moral Sentiments

We are now able to see exactly how the structures of the free-market undermine inclusive ethical debate. Ethical considerations about production, for example, are always tied to the self-interest of people employed in that production, since their livelihoods depend on it. Thus even when that production may be harming themselves and their community, it is difficult to have genuine ethical debate about the subject, because the overriding fear is that ethical action may result in pauperisation. The debate surrounding Sellafield, the nuclear reprocessing centre, sums this problem up clearly. Beatrix Campbell describes the problem:

> Sellafield is sustained not by science but by politics. A formidable and needy coalition defends it against its scientific sceptics, its green critics and its neighbours like Vivien Hope and Elizabeth Reay: key components are the constituency's Labour MP, Jack Cunningham, and the trade unions. The Federation of Women's Institutes has been bolder in its critique of the nuclear industries than the labour movement. There is no Silkwood at Sellafield.[43]

When vital personal interest is deliberately ranged against ethical action, it takes extraordinary character to overcome the temptation to rationalise our non-ethical behaviour. However, the provision of ethical goods and services might be thought to overcome this problem, since ethical considerations are being incorporated into the overall aim of production.

Whilst any instance of this thought of ethical choice is valuable, when it exists within a free-market system, it is not sufficient to meet our criterion fully. Ethical services, such as banking, and products, such as free-range eggs or fair-trade goods, incur extra costs precisely because they deviate from Acton's formula of buying cheap and selling dear. This results in ethical products being more expensive, and ethical services less attractive.

This reintroduces the idea that personal interest is ranged against morality, for now there must be a conscious decision to forgo personal consumption in return for ethical outcomes. This might seem like a curious statement to make, since it appears to be suggesting that when ethical action is ranged against self-interest, self-interest usually prevails. This would raise the question of how these ethical goods and services come to be produced in the first place. However, the problem is not simply that the structure of the ethical choice is antagonistic, it is that ethical choice through consumption becomes very much more problematic for those who have less income. The problem therefore is that since ethical goods are more expensive, it becomes easy for the rich to express their ethical beliefs, but it is a very much greater proposition if buying free-range eggs (often costing double their battery-produced alternatives) is at the expense of other necessary foodstuffs.

Other problems surround the idea of making and expressing ethical choice through market mechanisms. At the point of consumption, and therefore ethical choice, we exist as isolated individuals or families. As we have pointed out, it is difficult for isolated, partial, individuals to make genuine ethical decisions because they are cut off from the inclusive ethical debate which would give them the necessary rounded view. How are we know which brand of crisps was produced by a corporation which was concerned with environmental factors and treating its employees correctly, without representations from environmental groups and trade unions? Given the absence of lobbyists in supermarket aisles, it is difficult to come to informed decisions when we consume.

The lack of comprehensive debate also makes it easy for corporations to claim ethical status without any real substance. The problems associated with the environmental labelling of goods serves as a good example of this problem.

A further problem is that the existence of ethical businesses does nothing to relieve the problems associated with normal business practices. It might be possible to claim the status of 'role models' but this does not seem adequate. Corporations run by managers to serve the financial interests of distant shareholders, especially institutional shareholders such as pension funds, seem not to be very susceptible to ethical issues.

This can be explained by reference to the institutional structure of corporations which demands, by law, that the interests of shareholders is the primary concern of managers. This is a vital point in the argument that markets create conditions which are unfavourable to moral action and so we shall explore it at some length.

Pension funds exist specifically to increase the savings of their members, and therefore, pension fund managers are obliged to get maximum returns by buying cheap and selling dear. Therefore, the chain of obligation from corporations to shareholders, to pension-fund managers, to savers, instils short-termist thinking which prevents ethical action by demanding profit-maximisation over periods in which the long-term benefits of ethical action cannot be appreciated. Studies of American financial markets, and the way they effect business decisions seem to support this viewpoint. The free-market model of shareholder authority, developed by Harvard Professor of Economics Michael Jensen, gives a prime example of this form of short-termism.

It was this model which led to the phenomenon of 'Leverage Buy Outs' (LBOs). This is where a group of investors forms itself into a corporation which buys all the shares in one firm, and then sets very high profitability targets ensuring that the highest possible dividend is then returned to those shareholders. Studies of the effects of LBOs are reported by Doug Henwood, for instance the LBO of Safeway's supermarket chain by the LBO corporation KKR.

> The deal, regarded as one of the leverage movement's great successes, bought $28 million in stock profits and $100 million in options to Safeway's top executives, $15 million to investment bankers, another $25 million to lawyers, and $60 million in up-front fees for KKR - and pay cuts and unemployment for Safeway workers. Falude's [the journalist whose study it was] tales of suicide, heart attack, impoverishment and despair among workers displaced after the buy out were nothing compared to 'long-run efficiency effects'.[44]

Further, the financial success of these deals attracted the pension-fund managers, and so KKR was backed by Prudential, Aetna, General Electric's pension fund, Metropolitan Life, J.P. Morgan, Northwest Mutual, and the Oregon, Washington, and Wisconsin state pension funds, all supported KKR in its dealings.[45]

This highlights the way in which the nature of corporate finance results in behaviour which is resistant to ethical sanctions. The structure of ownership and control is designed first and foremost to respect the profit motive. When the profit motive calls, it is has a siren effect.

Thus the structure of business ownership exerts strong resistance to ethical action, even where wider society manages to co-ordinate an ethical response. LBOs, and other hostile take-overs, have been the subject of much critical discussion on both sides of the Atlantic, and yet this has not prevented them ignoring sensitive issues such as deforestation. Henwood notes,

> Besides labour, nature too suffered from the buyout boom. In one study of 82 hostile take-over bids between 1984 and 1986, for example, an important target was lumber firms who were not cutting enough timber given the interest rate, the growth of trees, and the price path for timber. The infamous Maxxam take-over of Pacific Lumber was inspired by fallow old redwoods that the latter wouldn't cut. Maxxam, powered by junk [bonds], took over Pacific Lumber and liquidated the trees.[46]

Thus we can safely conclude that the structure of ownership is a barrier to ethical behaviour. Not only does it contribute to the social and geographical stratification which is a major factor in narrative fragmentation, but the structure of ownership itself leads to short-term, financial-only considerations, which are inimical to ethical action.

Our conclusion must be, therefore, that the market interpretation of the ethical criterion is unacceptable. The workings of free-markets prevent genuine ethical debate by fragmenting our collective experience, and instilling a sense of self-interest which places ethical decision making in competition with our potential income. Further, the ownership structure of corporations means that even when society does raise a collective moral voice, there are structural resistances to the implementation of these ideas. Free-market capitalism is a poor mechanism for ethical action because it cannot concentrate on moral criteria without becoming distracted by the siren call of the profit motive.

Conclusions

We have seen, therefore, that communitarianism can generate reasonable criteria which a free-market system comprehensively fails to meet. On this basis we can confidently assert that it cannot sustain a system which respects community. Its definition of interdependence is too instrumental to acknowledge the different types of relationship which community members feel for one another. Its claim to respect the way communities are formed and sustained through their narratives turns out to be no more than an attempt to privilege free-market narratives over other forms of economic organisation. It fails to account for the way in which a community requires common narratives in order to cohere by ignoring the manner in which the workings of markets fragment these narratives.

Finally, its claim to ethical behaviour fails to acknowledge that ethical action depends upon including everyone in a moral debate about what production is carried on, and how it is to be conducted. By ignoring the manner in which the normal behaviour of markets undermines the possibility of ethical decision making and implementation, they lose the possibility of having the moral sentiments of the community respected by the production process. Markets cannot sustain community because they place a vital element in the formation of communal narratives outside the control of the community, placing it jointly in the hands of corporate executives, whose only goal is profit, and consumers, whose isolated, partial knowledge cannot sustain a wide ethical vision.

Notes

1   For example, the most widely-known communitarian, Amitai Etzioni, has stated that communitarianism has no economic agenda. See Amitai Etzioni, 'Common Values', *New Statesman and Society* (12th May 1995).

2   This definition is taken from the one elaborated in my thesis, 'The Concept of Community in Political Theory'.

3   For more on narrative methodology see: Alasdair MacIntyre, *After Virtue* (London: Duckworth, 1981); Margaret Somers, 'The Narrative Construction of Identity', *Theory and Society*, Vol. 23, No. 5 (1994), 605-49; Donald Polkinghorne, *Narrative Knowing and the Human Sciences* (New York: State University of New York Press, 1988).

4   Raymond Plant, *Community and Ideology*, (London and Boston: Routledge, 1974), p. 28.

5   Robert Nozick, *Philosophical Investigations*, (Camb, Mass.: Harvard University Press, 1981), p. 395-6. He states, 'Intended personal influence on wrongdoing (hypnosis, psychosurgery etc.) are complete mitigating circumstances, because you are acting out the products of someone else's intentions, but impersonal (structural) causes do not mitigate in this way... When impersonal causes instil in a person the very same character traits [immoral ones]... it is his [the agent's] intentions that animate his actions, *for there is no better candidate available*' (my emphasis).

6   Adam Smith, from 'An Inquiry into the Nature and Causes of the Wealth of Nations', quoted in Bill Jordan, *The Common Good: Citizenship, Morality and Self-Interest* (Oxford: Basil Blackwell, 1989), p. 27.

7   F. A. Hayek, *The Fatal Conceit: The Errors of Socialism* (London: Routledge, 1988), p. 81; H.B. Acton, *The Morals of Markets*, (London: Longman, 1971), p. 15.

8   F. A. Hayek, *The Fatal Conceit: The Errors of Socialism*, p. 85.

9   For examples of this argument see, Acton, *The Morals of Markets*, pp. 62-3; Hayek, *The Fatal Conceit: The Errors of Socialism*, pp. 71-4.

10   J.K. Galbraith, *The Affluent Society* (Harmondsworth: Penguin, 1987), p. 98.

11   Galbraith, *The Affluent Society*, p. 127.

12   See, for example, David Miller, *Market, State, and Community* (Oxford: Clarendon Press, 1989), Chapter 5.

13   Hayek, *The Fatal Conceit: The Errors of Socialism*, p. 53-4.

14   Edward Gondolf, 'In Search of a Viable Community-Based Economic Organisation', *Human Organisation*, Vol. 47, No. 2 (1988), p. 154.

15   Hayek, *The Fatal Conceit: The Errors of Socialism*, p. 32.

16   For example, United States covert operations in Honduras and Nicaragua. For details see Noam Chomsky, *Deterring Democracy*, (New York: Hill and Wang, 1992).

17   Hayek, *The Fatal Conceit: The Errors of Socialism*, p. 51.

18   Hayek, *The Fatal Conceit: The Errors of Socialism*, p. 56.

19   Hayek, *The Fatal Conceit: The Errors of Socialism*, p. 54.

20   Fred Block and Margaret Somers, 'Beyond the Economistic Fallacy: The Holistic Social Science of Karl Polanyi', in Theda Skocpol ed., *Vision and Method in Historical Sociology*, (Cambridge and New York: Cambridge University Press, 1984), p. 56.

21   Block and Somers, 'Beyond the Economistic Fallacy: The Holistic Social Science of Karl Polanyi', p. 57.

22   Acton, *The Morals of Markets*, p. 61.

23   Robert Nozick, *Anarchy, State, and Utopia* (New York: Basic Books, 1974), p. 302.

24   Nozick, *Anarchy, State, and Utopia*, pp. 32-3.

25   Nozick, *Anarchy, State, and Utopia*, p. 22.

26   Nozick, *Anarchy, State, and Utopia*, p. 22.

27   Nozick, *Anarchy, State, and Utopia*, p. 19.

28   Hayek, *The Fatal Conceit: The Errors of Socialism*, p. 74. See also p. 71, and p. 73.

29   Nozick, *Anarchy, State, and Utopia*, p. 32.

30   Acton, *The Morals of Markets*, pp. 6-12.

31   Acton, *The Morals of Markets*, pp. 16-19.

32   Shell Petroleum Development Company of Nigeria Limited, *Nigeria Brief: The Ogoni Issue*, (1995), p. 2.

33   Cyril Obi, 'Globalisation and Local Resistance: The Case of Ogoni vs. Shell', *New Political Economy*, Vol. 2, No. 1 (1997), p. 142.

34   The source for this information is Geoffrey Lean, "Shell 'Paid Nigerian Military' ", *The Independent on Sunday*, 17th December 1995.

35   Lean, "Shell 'Paid Nigerian Military' ".

36   It is necessary to point out that Shell is not a special case of business acting unethically. Other companies such as Elf and Agip are also involved with the Nigerian government in oil production, and British Petroleum has had similar disputes with indigenous peoples in its operations in South America.

37   Acton, *The Morals of Markets*, pp. 19-25.

38   Hayek, *The Fatal Conceit: The Errors of Socialism*, p. 70.

39   Hayek, *The Fatal Conceit: The Errors of Socialism*, p. 68.

40   Nozick, *Philosophical Investigations*, p. 514.

41   Nozick, *Anarchy, State, and Utopia*, p. 352.

42   Acton, *The Morals of Markets*, p. 13.

43   Beatrix Campbell, *The Independent*, 13 October 1993.

44   Doug Henwood, *Wall St: How It Works and For Whom* (London: Verso, 1997), p. 273-4. Will Hutton makes a similar critique of British financial institutions in *The State We're In* (London: Vintage, 1995).

45   Henwood, *Wall St: How It Works and For Whom*, p. 272.

46   Henwood, *Wall St: How It Works and For Whom*, p. 274.

PART II
THE MARKET AND
SOCIAL INSTITUTIONS

6   The Ethical Effects of Privatisation

BARBARA GOODWIN

Privatisation denotes *the transfer to a commercial organisation of the right and duty to provide services or goods previously provided by a public sector organisation*. In Britain, we recently experienced a series of Conservative administrations (1979-1996) committed to the ideology of private enterprise and to shrinking the public sector. Whichever nationally owned enterprises could conveniently be privatised, were; some parts of the civil service unsuitable for privatisation were transformed into quasi-autonomous 'executive agencies'; other parts of the public sector were instructed to contract out some of their functions and to emulate the customer-orientation of business by adopting 'Citizens' Charters'. The National Health Service [NHS] was required to construct an 'internal market' dividing its functions between those of purchasers and providers [see Descombes in this volume].

This chapter is based on qualitative, interview-based research in five organisations of which two had been privatised, one is a quasi-autonomous government agency and two are still in the public sector. After a short review of arguments about the ethical nature of business (Section 1), I use my research findings in ex-public-sector organisations to illustrate the ethical effects of privatisation on the *public service ethos* and then contrast these with my findings in two Local Authorities (Section 2). Section 3 focuses on the damaging ethical effects of the continuing process of 'marketisation' in some public services. Finally, I argue that, although the attitudinal findings suggest that privatisation has not had adverse ethical effects in the organisations that I studied, there are inbuilt conflicts of interest between the stakeholders of business organisations which may make it undesirable to extend the privatisation process further.

1. Business and Ethics

Is business in itself less ethical than the public sector? Left-wing thinkers have sometimes maintained that the extraction of profit is unethical because of exploitation of the workforce by extraction of surplus value, but the general consensus in liberal capitalist countries is that profits are not essentially unethical. R.H.Tawney, no friend of capitalism, traces this conviction back to Calvinism which 'set the profits of trade and finance...on the same level of respectability as the earnings of the labourer and the rents of the landlord'. He quotes Calvin: 'What reason is there why the income from business should not be larger than that from landowning? Whence do the merchant's profits come, except from his own diligence and industry?'[1] Contemporary debate usually focuses on *profit levels* and the contentious issue of 'fat cats' rather than the principle of profit itself - if that were questioned, it would subvert the whole business enterprise. The principle of profit is raised again in the last section of this chapter. I now turn to two questions particularly relevant to the privatisation debate, which are (i) whether business has social responsibilities and (ii) whether businesses are more inclined to behave unethically than public-sector (government) organisations.

The idea that business has social responsibilities has been hotly disputed by some economists and business ethicists, most famously Milton Friedman, who wrote in 1962:

> There is one and only one social responsibility of business - to use its resources and engage in activities designed to increase its profits so long as it stays *within the rules of the game*...[2]

Elaine Sternberg, author of *Just Business* (1994) believes that Friedman does not go far enough. Her own position has a Nozickian slant - she argues that using business resources for non-business purposes is *theft*, 'an unjustified appropriation of the owners' property'.[3] This, she thinks, is true however worthy the non-business purposes are, even for charitable contributions. Sternberg's book received a rather frosty reception from writers on business ethics. But to the extent that she and Friedman contend that businesses have no obligation to pursue ethical goals for their own sake, we can hardly quarrel with them. A business is not a charity. We can however maintain as a minimum requirement that businesses have a social obligation to pursue their goal, whether that be maximisation of profit, turnover or market share, *in an ethical way* - for example, to treat shareholders, customers, employees and competitors fairly. This point was endorsed by Friedman when he defined the 'rules of the game' as being to 'engage in open and free competition, without deception or fraud'. We might call this the 'minimalist ethic' of business.

However, there have been attempts to argue that business and markets have ethical qualities beyond the mere 'rules of the game' - for example, the argument derived from classical economics that bad firms (i.e. inefficient or *unethical* firms) will be driven out of business. This view gives rise to the maxim 'Good ethics is good business'. Another argument states that markets are conducive to individual freedom and autonomy, which are in themselves morally good. This is reminiscent of J. S. Mill's contention that even if government could provide services for citizens better than those which they can provide themselves or obtain through a market system, its *not* doing so educates people to provide things for themselves and promotes self-reliance.[4] These ethical arguments for the market have been debated by John Gray, Raymond Plant, Allen Buchanan and others.[5]

A different attempt to demonstrate that business has an intrinsically moral quality is found in Jane Jacobs' *Systems of Survival* (1993). She claims to explain the moral foundations of society by looking back to early human communities which survived either by 'taking' - hunting, foraging, pillaging - or by trading. Jacobs suggests that these different ways of life gave rise to opposed values, the guardian and the commercial syndrome. The 'guardian syndrome' is the government syndrome - based on loyalty, obedience, tradition, hierarchy and 'strategic deception' - deception in the interests of a wider strategy. Its raison d'être is, at bottom, territorial defence and aggrandisement. By contrast, the 'commercial syndrome' requires honesty, competition and respect for contracts. It promotes efficiency, industriousness, inventiveness and shuns the use of force. Jacobs argues that *commerce* is the locus of moral purity - she says that government is 'essentially barbaric' while business is fundamentally ethical.[6]

Similar views about the essential moral qualities of business were held by some early commentators on industrialism. For example, the utopian socialist Saint-Simon believed that the growth of industrialism would bring about an era of peace and tranquillity, since the *chefs d'industrie* ('captains of industry'), when given political power, would promote harmony between nations, in strong contrast to the warring nationalism of Europe in the eighteenth and nineteenth centuries.[7] Jacobs' argument is based on an eccentric characterisation of government which does not match modern liberal democracies very well; her characterisation of commerce nevertheless carries some conviction, because global capitalism evidently prospers best in peacetime and in a free-trade climate. Government depends on the territorial sovereignty of the nation state, while business and commerce are international and require peace and the removal of trade barriers between countries. This point, also made two centuries ago by Saint-Simon, is well illustrated by the development of the European Union since its inception in 1958 as the European Economic Community (EEC), originally an association based on trade in coal and steel. If we substitute 'business' where Jacobs uses 'commerce', the argument is that business has valuable ethical qualities of its own, for example in promoting peace and honest, open dealing.

Taken at its face value, this argument supports the view that business enterprises are in themselves no less ethical than public sector enterprises (although either equally might become corrupt or behave unethically on occasion). However, the Friedman-Sternberg argument suggests that the social responsibilities of businesses are limited to fairness and playing by the (market) rules; this minimalist ethic leads us to question whether the private sector is a suitable provider of any public, welfare-related service where an element of supererogation is important.

2. Privatisation and the Public Service Ethos

If we accept that business is no less ethical *in principle* than government enterprise, is there anything which distinguishes public-sector organisations ethically from business, in practical terms? This question is usually answered by reference to the attitudes of public-sector employees and the values espoused within public-sector organisations: there is said to be a *public service ethos* [PSE]. What is the public service ethos? It is not the business ethic of satisfying the customer but rather what the sociologist Max Weber characterised as *impersonality* - an ethos of un-self-interested, impartial dealing with people plus the application of rules, in a context uncontaminated by the drive for profit. Furthermore, it embodies the idea of doing what is best for the client or 'customer', possibly in a paternalistic way, which may involve telling the client what is good for her. The PSE connotes an element of altruism and perhaps even of supererogation. Ideally, the PSE characterises the attitude of the *professional* administrator whose own job does not depend on the customer's response or satisfaction but who does that job because he or she cares for the wellbeing of the client or customer. Critics might argue that the PSE is a myth used to justify the existence of self-satisfied bureaucrats. My own research suggests that public-service employees think differently.

My purpose here is to ask what happens in practice to the PSE when public-sector organisations are privatised or quasi-privatised. I answer this question on the basis of research data gathered from in-depth, semi-structured interviews with a cross-section of employees and managers in five organisations. The interviews focused on their moral attitudes and ethical dilemmas.[8] Two of the organisations were fully privatised, a national airline and a water company; the executive agency (a quasi-autonomous 'government agency' also sometimes referred to as a 'Next Steps Agency') was created in the early 1990s. Has privatisation changed the ethos of the privatised companies, because they are profit-driven? Has it changed the ethos of the quasi-privatised Agency because targets, budgets, and performance indicators [PIs] must be met in the new business-orientated organisation? How have those public service providers which remain in the public sector been affected by 'marketisation'? The following sub-sections indicate my findings.

Beyond the Public Service Ethos - the Airline

The Airline was privatised early in 1983 - so thoroughly privatised that employees can hardly remember when it ceased to be state-owned! Although many of the people I interviewed had worked there before privatisation (the average length of service was 16.5 years), none mentioned a previous public service ethos. However, there was an unusually strong emphasis on *customer service* and also a pride in professional conduct. Many of the participants' personal moral beliefs were 'other-related' - more so than in some organisations that I worked with - which may have been because of close cooperation between colleagues and the extensive interaction with customers. An airline is an unusual enterprise: whereas many businesses can keep customers at arm's length, a large number of airline staff have to 'live with' their customers for long periods, for example during flights or during delays at airports, so that good customer relations and good service delivery are essential both for a congenial working life and for business success. This may help to explain the other-orientated moral values subscribed to by the participants in my study. Also, recruitment and promotion doubtless favour those with good interpersonal skills and high personal standards. (A more venal explanation would be that airlines compete fiercely on customer service and that this is therefore inculcated into all staff.) Another ethically interesting aspect of the airline business is that many staff are literally in the same boat as customers; any threat to the safety or comfort of passengers also threatens colleagues. This reinforces the operation of the moral Golden Rule in which many participants believed: treat others as you would wish to be treated. Your own life, as well as the lives of your fellow-employees and customers, may be at risk if work is not properly done. Doing your best for customers equals doing your best for yourself and your colleagues.

Many of an airline's duties are legally prescribed, especially where safety is concerned. The airline in question had gone beyond legal regulation by voluntarily introducing a Code of Conduct which encompasses conduct within the organisation and business behaviour generally. Although most participants believed that they themselves would follow the Code's principles automatically - for example, they would be fair and honest - the Code may be useful, in that it reaches parts of the organisation which government regulation may not reach. However, the Code is not *the same as* a PSE - and many private companies have adopted Codes, as an emblem of purity. Overall, the participants in my study showed a keen sensitivity to customers' needs, but their customers are not vulnerable in the way that customers of many public-sector organisations - for example, the National Health Service - are, in the sense that they are able to afford to fly (however, some passengers are vulnerable, or unhappy about air travel). The customer-service orientation therefore differs from the PSE in public-sector organisations, since it is promoted by the company in order to supply a good product to paying customers. But if the staff of the Airline believe in customer service, treat others as they would themselves wish to be treated and always act professionally, the end result may be the same in the terms of customer treatment and satisfaction.

Water - a Company in Transition

The participants who had worked in the Water Company prior to privatisation in 1989 all agreed that the company had improved since privatisation, but some had reservations about the side-effects such as commercialisation, constant reorganisation and redundancies. Significantly, they were divided on the desirability of retaining a PSE in the new company.[9] Those critical of the PSE thought it had always been a sham; however, they strongly maintained that *good customer service* was just as crucial to business and was not the sole preserve of public sector organisations.

I've been struck by how strong the public service ethic is. Although we get

100

bad publicity sometimes, there's a strong feeling that we're giving a public service. In any crisis people turn out. There's a paternalistic feeling of public service.

When I began I used to take it as a personal affront if people were without water. It's the public service ethos - we've spent 9 years trying to get rid of it!

I worked for the [old] Water Board. People joined it because it had a public service feeling - plodders, undynamic people. When I came back the atmosphere was very different. People with 'serving the community' values would not fit in.

There's still a public service ethos - sometimes too little, sometimes too much. The Chairman talked of the strength of the mongrel marriage between old public-service and new entrepreneurial personnel. There's a commercial edge -when I talk about it, it slightly offends public service ethics.

Some people use the public service ethic as an excuse for [lacking] energy/drive/change, so it's a plus quality and a negative.

I think the 'public service ethos' is lip service. In industry we had to serve the customer too.

*We [need to] change some of the people with the public sector ethic, which lies too thick in some places. Your idleness was pinned on the sense of respectability of what you were doing. Before privatisation this was a dinosaur of a company! But **the main object of a utility business is still to serve customers**.*

Public service ethos? The quicker it goes, the better for the customer. It meant "we do it when we feel good about it, but we don't do it all the time".
[The Chief Executive]

In contrast to these upbeat comments, there were plenty of stories about the company's hardline policies on debt collection, enforced through disconnection of domestic water supplies. Employees were sent to training courses about how much the company lost because of defaulting customers, to insulate them against over-sympathising with those who had to be disconnected. There were also tales of attempts to cause customers to pay for repairs which were the company's responsibility. However, it was said repeatedly that most workers who dealt with the public would try to bend the rules for vulnerable customers, such as the elderly, or when they felt that the company was shirking its responsibilities. Was that a remnant of the PSE? Overall, Water staff were sceptical of the PSE (especially at the management level, where it was perceived as a thing of the past and an obstacle to commercial success and enterprise), while remaining aware that they were delivering an essential service to people, to whom they owed a duty of care.

A Hybrid Organisation - the Agency

This is a large agency involved in the distribution of welfare benefits which attained executive agency status in the early 1990s. It was formerly part of the Department of Social Security [DSS]. Executive agencies are typically run more like businesses: they are concerned with costs and targets and are run by chief executives. Participants were asked if the Agency has a public service ethos and whether becoming an executive agency has made any difference to staff attitudes. Most said that there was a PSE, although a few questioned whether it was genuine or merely expedient. However, most were enthusiastic about the changes brought about by the creation of the Agency. *A better attitude to customers* was the most frequently mentioned improvement (by 50% of the participants) and some people specifically mentioned the Agency's Customer Charter (a quarter). Their comments indicated that real and tangible improvement had occurred:

> *Many years ago, if you were serving a customer it was a secondary issue.*

> *In the 1960s people thought it was a fine job, if only there weren't customers.*

> *In the 1960s, the pace was slower...no-one gave a damn for the customer, except for having normal human concern for some of them. There was no question of anyone who was rude to a customer being rebuked. We did not put ourselves out for customers, it was very bureaucratic and we required customers to put everything in writing.*

> *Customers are treated better than before, they're respected more by staff. But the majority of staff are not the 'old school', the old civil service.*

> *When the Agency was set up it took a strong line on customer service - before that, **we** told customers what they needed!*

However, some speakers pointed out (rightly) that customers have no choice about using the Agency and one said that the new *business ethos* worked to the detriment of customers:

> We're part of the welfare state, like the NHS, and should be proud to work for it. But some people aren't, and feel as if they're there to stop people getting benefits. It may be coming from the management **trying to run this as a business**.

Greater accountability for budgets and targets, the Quality Framework and greater emphasis on good value for the taxpayer (eliminating fraud, for example) were also mentioned as proof of an improved service ethos, although one employee said that the anti-fraud drive could harm new customers (who must be visited at home before any benefits can be paid, which takes time). Several participants felt that the political agenda was detrimental to the PSE:

> There is a public service ethos but because of the political links it can't always be genuine. It is always playing to the political gallery: if it is seen to be right to be good to the customer, we will be.

> [The Agency is] trying to have a public service ethos, but at the end of the day you have to do things which are morally dodgy, like stopping money to 16 and 17-year-olds. There are pressures to save money...We have a target for fraud, which seems odd and is perhaps a moral issue.

The new business orientation had caused some moral dilemmas - three participants had been asked by managers to falsify statistics to meet targets. There was a general feeling that the Agency is an ethically concerned organisation and that most (although not all) individual staff are ethically aware and keen to help customers: many persist in what can be a stressful job because they wish to help the vulnerable.

The 'Old' Public Service Ethos - Two Local Authorities

I carried out similar studies in two Local Authorities [LAs] in London: both were run by Labour Councils. By contrast with participants from the organisations discussed above, local government officers [LGOs] largely rejected the possibility of private-sector provision of local services. All the participants had a clear and explicit sense of public commitment tempered with some dismay at the way in which governments had treated local

103

government since the mid-1980s, by curtailing their powers and resources - although participants stated that the greater efficiency and accountability were improvements. Virtually all thought there was a PSE in their Authorities, although several thought it was under threat. There was a strong sense that 'business is different'. Many contrasted their organisations with profit-driven business:

> *The private sector is in it for money and has no moral responsibility - they will look at the bottom line. If the [council] tax function is put out to contract, will they have sympathy for the non-payers?*

> *Local authorities are dedicated to helping the community rather than helping their own pockets, like commercial organisations.*

> *The thing about local government recently is that standards of moral probity must be higher, more is expected of people if they work here - more perhaps than in the private sector.*

Other features which, they thought, distinguish commercial enterprise from LAs were the public accountability and democracy in the latter, the fact that LAs provide services which enhance living standards and emphasise quality, and their duty to provide basic services whether profitable or not.

> *A Company will invest or disinvest in certain areas as it suits them, but LAs have a duty to invest in certain areas. There is a public service ethos here, but not as something totally altruistic - it's just that people enjoy the job. The public service ethos is a way of doing things and looking at things.*

> *There is an inner dedication to serving the public. You feel you are doing something to improve services. The managers and people at the operational level are dedicated.*

Participants who had also worked in the private sector were not so convinced (or complacent) about the PSE: one, who had been used to working long hours in business, commented critically that people did not work so hard in the Authority.

Overall, there was a close match between the participants' perceptions of their own responsibilities to the public and their perception of the attitude of the Council and the Authority as a whole. There may be an element of self-selection in all this, since conscientious people would probably not work for an organisation which they considered socially or ethically irresponsible. One said 'if you don't have a public service ethos you wouldn't be working here' and another, 'I have my own political views and I wouldn't work with just *any* local authority. There is a moral feeling about this authority'.

Reservations about changes in local government were expressed, however, with frequent references to the resource constraints which result, particularly, from rate-capping: staff were working under greater pressure as a result, job security had been lost and there was some feeling (although this was not universal) that LAs no longer looked after their staff properly. The arrival of CCT (discussed in detail below), had forced participants to reflect on the difference between business and the public services, and they offered the following comparisons:

(i) LAs provide a monopoly service, so 'customers' have no choice;
(ii) LAs suffer from legal and financial regulations which do not apply to companies and so cannot compete or show initiative as businesses can;
(iii) unlike businesses, LAs have no incentives and no clear success indicators, and
(iv) the private sector is more positive and encouraging to staff.

Local Authorities may not be able to behave wholly like businesses, but the Citizens' Charter movement was a government attempt to make such public service providers simulate the supposed pro-customer attitude of business. (Plant argues that in fact Charters were intended to redistribute power 'from professional groups to the consumer of professional services outside the market sector'.[10]) The Charters have indeed made LA clients behave more like *customers*. Several participants remarked that the public now has different expectations about LAs, which some would see as good (and as empowerment of the public) and some as regrettable.

People now have different expectations, they expect that organisations will **serve** *them. I'm totally against all these Charters, but I think they're having an effect.*

*The "**Me** society" means we have a more aggressive clientele and has changed the way we go about our jobs. We can get challenged because people pursue selfish objectives against the will of the community and they use local government to do it.*

Morale was not very high in these LAs, and constant reorganisation and some (earlier) redundancies made for feelings of insecurity. Escalating government demands for new service provision without extra funding, the requirements of the Citizens' Charter and the greater assertiveness of 'customers': all these were making the work of LGOs more demanding. Yet virtually all the participants in these studies expressed a strong commitment to public service and to helping the most vulnerable or needy sections of their communities and many, additionally, had 'political' ideals such as increasing equality and social justice. Whether such commitment and aspirations can survive the process of CCT is discussed in the next section.

3. The Marketisation of the Public Sector

Many public services have been forced to become 'hybrid' organisations - with a mixture of public-sector and private-sector elements - because of the recent Conservative governments' policies on market testing and contracting out, and compulsory competitive tendering [CCT] in the case of LAs. Do these half-measures, which we might call the 'marketisation' of the public sector (falling short of full privatisation), create ethical problems? What do employees feel about the ethics and the outcomes of these processes?

CCT in Local Authorities

Compulsory competitive tendering requires LAs to put out a certain proportion of their services to tender. LA departments can tender against commercial companies to run the services and since their bids need not include a profit element, they may succeed in keeping the work in-house. The CCT process raises a number of moral issues and many LA employees disagree with it on ideological grounds. The process also raises issues about the control and accountability of contractors, service quality and the effect on staff in terms of redundancies or poorer working conditions. Some participants in my two LA studies worked in areas unaffected by CCT while others were affected, e.g. those in 'Direct Services', which include services like park maintenance, traffic control and rubbish collection. (For many LAs, Direct Services have been the most obvious Department to subject to CCT.) In one LA it was an open secret that the Labour administration was politically committed to keeping the services subject to CCT in-house wherever possible; the second Authority was, less overtly, trying to do the same. Employees were divided on the desirability of holding this line in all cases. One manager suggested that it was only the *core duties*, the welfare-related duties, which should be kept in house, while functions like security could well be contracted out. Adverse comments were made on the actual CCT process itself, on the timetable set by government and on its effects on the Authority.

> *It's having an effect on the way the Authority works because so much is divided into client/contractor. We spend a lot of time and resources on setting up CCT and it seems to lead to some duplication. I'm not sure that the end-product is necessarily better.*

> *I don't necessarily agree with changing contractors for change's sake because the tendering process costs money and time and the change can disrupt the service.*

> *CCT is not a moral problem for me but a managerial problem: it wastes a lot of time, there is a lot of paperwork and bureaucracy. What it was designed to do, to improve the performance of local government, was achieved years ago and it is now counterproductive.*

Attitudes to the principle of CCT varied: some participants argued that privately-run services would be inferior to those offered by LAs; that they would be less humanely run; that the cheapest way of doing something, which the tendering system encourages, is not always the best. Using outside contractors might put vulnerable people at risk:

> *Sheltered housing caretaking could be put out to tender but the service might be less good; unless the contract specified in detail that the caretaker should visit each house every day, it wouldn't get done.*

> *I can understand why it's happening for reasons I've already mentioned [increasing efficiency etc.] but giving the contracts to people who charge the least means they will probably give a less good service. Relationships between the private contractor and the client [the LA] would be less good than they are with my Department. We do a lot more for the Council, but the contractors would just do what's in the contract, end of story.* [A Direct Services employee]

> *I have moral misgivings about it because it would lead to worse services. If you have a contract saying "We'll do X, Y and Z" it would mean you **only** do X, Y and Z.*

We should not assume that Local Authorities do things better than anyone else; choice is a good idea. There are a lot of good voluntary organisations, but there are also people who are crooks setting up private children's homes. I've just had to remove four children from a [private] home.

Some participants also stated the benefits of CCT in the same breath:

I think CCT has helped with the provision of services; it makes sure people do their jobs. In the past things got put off, delayed, because people were going sick and fiddling the system.

It has made a difference to office organisation; people used to be laid back, relying on good will.

Deterioration of conditions for the workforce was also a major concern for a number of participants:

I don't think my job is at risk under CCT but my terms and conditions would be worse, I'd probably have to work longer hours, which really means a cut in pay.

If you can only win bids by cutting hours, wages and conditions of service, I say 'Don't bother'.

With CCT they are going to have an awful shock. We have set up groups to tender for the business; but people will not wish to start work at 8am and take a pay cut. An outside company tendering for the work will expect workers to do that and will treat workers like zombies. If the in-house bid succeeds, people like me will have to take pay cuts.

I know that the in-house cleaning bid was unrealistic, they could not do the things they said in the time allowed. That makes the whole contract thing seem dishonest. The office cleaner talks about deterioration, cuts, her anxiety about her job, and she's distressed by not being able to do the job as she'd like to.

The success of in-house bids raised practical and ethical problems. Some people felt that the political will to ensure in-house success did not always lead to the most efficient outcome because, for example, a large number of staff had to be involved in monitoring the contracts. Monitoring any contractor is time-consuming and it raises strategic (and moral) dilemmas when the contractor is in-house.

> *I can say things to the [in-house] teams which I would not say to an external contractor, but I'm also limited because they are part of the organisation. For example, if I wanted to sack them I would have to think very carefully indeed about the consequences and implications.*

> *Our contractors are all in-house, which makes monitoring harder: if it were a commercial organisation, we'd have more power. It does not do the Council much good if we are over-critical.*

The propriety of the secret tender process with in-house bids was also mentioned:

> *Although the tender process is secret, there is inevitably some seepage through the Chinese wall of information about who else is bidding for a contract.*

Most participants shared the view that CCT could 'go too far', but some also said that it had initially had some good effects and had shown that local government was not a monopoly.

Some regretted that LAs were moving in a commercial direction and thought that CCT blurred the distinction between local government and business. The major problem in privatising some of the 'caring' services was generally agreed to be that companies would only carry out contracts 'to the letter' - as philosophers might say, there are no acts of supererogation in the commercial world. Given that the stereotype of the bureaucrat is of someone who carries out rules 'to the letter', this distinction made by many participants was significant: it suggested that they did *not* see themselves as bureaucrats, but rather as public servants, informed by the PSE and with a duty to help the community. They feared that CCT would mean poorer service to customers, many of whom are vulnerable.

Market Testing in the Agency

The Agency was described earlier as a hybrid organisation - a part of the public sector being run rather like a business. A further move towards commercial principles is in train. The privatisation of some functions has become part of the Agency's management strategy, partly because of (Conservative) government directives, partly because it is seen as a means of

109

cost-cutting or ensuring more effective performance. When I asked participants 'What do you think are the greatest risks for the Agency?' two-thirds replied that privatisation and market-testing presented the greatest risks.

Participants felt vehemently about this. It was not just a case of old-style civil servants in revolt against new developments, because most of them had welcomed the creation of the Agency and compared it favourably with the DSS. Key complaints were that market-testing was costly and inefficient, 'a political sham' and 'a total shambles'. Privatisation would have *ethical effects*, being harmful to the PSE ('there won't be the good will shown by the staff') and to claimants, as the following comments show:

> *If [privatisation] happens, I believe the strong public service ethos, the moral part, will be under threat...There has to be a decision whether the needs of the public or of the taxpayer are greater. The emphasis is still on the customer, rightly I think, because the people who use our service are more vulnerable and this is what keeps us on their side. If we were a privatised organisation there will be a greater drag towards efficiency. I also have concerns about safeguards. In the past I saw customers being abused by individual power-holders. I have a fear that such behaviour could return under privatisation. Wherever you are dealing with people who lack power there's risk of abuse.*

> *All our office facilities (including security) are contracted out. If you talk to their staff, they are very discontented and are leaving. We won't get a very good service. Our staff, when subjected to the market testing preparation, are often demoralised and demotivated.*

> *Would an external agency have the insight and knowledge to deal with such work?*

> *I'm not convinced that a company whose intention is to make a profit is the best agency to deliver this service.*

> *We find here that the privatised services are far worse than they were...we've been out of claims forms for three weeks because of the contractor's problems.*

The participants' fears of increased privatisation were by no means groundless: in 1997 three business consortia were invited by the government to 'shadow' Agency work for a year. 'If any of them can demonstrate ways of providing better value for money and improving the quality of service for

110

clients, it will be considered as a candidate to take over management of benefit offices.'[11]

4. Does Privatisation Have Adverse Ethical Effects?

My research suggests that the attitudes of employees in the particular privatised or quasi-autonomous organisations which I studied were not significantly ethically different from those of employees in the public sector who claimed to be animated by a public service ethos. The language might differ, with more reference to *customer service* in Airline and Water (and also in the Agency, where ex-DSS employees emphasised that customer service had improved), but the ideal of professionalism was common to many employees of all these organisations, even those working in relatively menial roles. However, the research did reveal considerable resistance to creeping privatisation among most remaining public-sector employees in the Agency and the Local Authorities. This resistance could be attributed to innate conservatism or to job protectionism, but the interview material (some of which is quoted above) indicates that they perceived a clear ethical problem: when vital services are provided by companies and employees without any tradition of PSE, and provided 'to the letter' of the contract, those services may deteriorate and people may suffer harm. That is a major danger of privatisation.

Those warnings bring us back to the question of whether commercial enterprise are intrinsically less ethical than the public services, as the public-sector participants feared. If that fear is justified, further privatisation of public services should arouse anxieties. But if *large* public and private sector organisations operate similarly, does it matter which runs the public services? (The case of small contractors is different: they may be more inclined to cut corners and less inclined towards professionalism.) Section 1 above outlined the argument that business has ethical qualities of its own. In this final section, I will argue that there are intrinsic reasons why private enterprise might be less ethical in providing public services than public-sector organisations.

Certainly, we should not exaggerate the differences between business and public sector organisations: *both* have stewardship of someone else's money (shareholders' money or taxpayers'). Charles Handy has argued powerfully for the stewardship role of companies,[12] just as the House of Commons Public Accounts Committee repeatedly makes the point about the stewardship role of public bodies. The Nolan Committee and the Cadbury

111

Report have made similar points about the importance of accountability in the public and private sectors. Both sectors offer services to customers, although the motivation for doing so may be different, i.e. to help people or to make profit. The great difference is that the customers of the Agency, of Local Authorities and of the Water Company have no exit option. This is why these captive 'customers' need guarantees of good treatment - the PSE was usually thought to offer such a guarantee and Customers' (Citizens') Charters now afford a written guarantee.

Another common feature is that both types of organisation must take account of their *stakeholders*. There has been much debate recently about the stakeholder concept, debate directed at encouraging more ethical behaviour in organisations. But stakeholders are not one homogeneous group: in the private sector, there is a divergence of interests between the customer, the employee and the shareholder, and conflicts of interest also occur in public-sector organisations. Better treatment of one stakeholder group can damage the interests of others: for example, in the case of water companies, there is a *shareholders vs. customers* conflict of interests. The drive for profits has disadvantaged captive customers through higher water charges - and, insult to injury, water profits are so high that they have become a national scandal. Another area of conflict is *customers vs. employees*. When senior management at the Agency decided that offices should open at 8.30am instead of 9.00am for the convenience of customers, employees were inconvenienced and disgruntled, especially as there was no demonstrated demand for earlier opening. The Citizens' Charters in LAs have also disadvantaged employees to the extent that they have had to change working practices and work harder. In general, employees in the private Airline and Water Company and the quasi-autonomous Agency felt that their new employers were less caring to employees than previously.

Is there always a zero-sum game between stakeholder groups? If, in business, promoting the interests of customers or shareholders always detracts from the wellbeing of employees, and satisfying the shareholders always detracts from the wellbeing of customers (or vice versa), what possibility is there of equally ethical and just behaviour to all three groups? The utilitarian might argue that maximising consumption and customer satisfaction maximises profits and simultaneously maximises the wellbeing of the company's employees (i.e. they can be paid more). But this optimistic scenario ignores the stakeholders' conflicts of interest. It also makes an assumption of almost unlimited demand which is often false. People may want to be able to shop at their supermarket 24 hours a day, but they will not buy

112

three times as much food because opening hours have extended. Water consumption also presumably has natural limits and in any case the resource itself is finite. Similarly, while some benefits claimants might favour visiting the benefits office early, earlier opening does not cause *more* people to claim benefits. In economic terms, benefits and water are special kinds of goods, with (respectively) inelastic or relatively inelastic demand,[13] which falsify market assumptions about universal simultaneous maximisation. The Airline is a case of an inelastic *supplier* (in the short term at least) - it cannot conjure up extra planes and landing slots from nowhere if a load of extra customers arrive - and so it will also not satisfy the optimistic 'simultaneous maximisation' formula. In the end, even with 'typical' firms and products, the utilitarian's optimistic outcome is unlikely to be achieved, and one stakeholder group will benefit at another's expense. The ethical problem with the privatisation of public services is that the conflict of interests is more likely to be resolved in the shareholders' interest than in the (captive) customers' interests. That is a second danger of privatisation: it is not simply that the cost of privatised services will have to include profits and may therefore be higher, but that in any conflict-of-interest situation the company will be almost bound to settle the conflict in favour of shareholders (unless it faces serious and immediate competition from other would-be providers, which has not been the case in many privatisations).

For and Against Privatisation

The reasons stated publicly for privatisation in the 1980s were efficiency and greater responsiveness to customers. There were also ideological reasons, such as shrinking the public sector, and creating a 'shareholder democracy'. There were also highly pragmatic reasons, one being to avoid using taxpayers' money to rescue services such as the water system which had suffered chronic under-investment; another was to make money out of 'selling off the family silver', in Lord Macmillan's famous phrase. No claim was made, as far as I know, that exposure to the market would make the privatised utilities and services more *ethical*. But one might try to construct an ethical argument in favour of privatisation as follows:

Suppose that customer service and responsiveness to customers are (morally) good in themselves. Then, privatisation will be good if the following conditions are satisfied:

(i) it is proved beyond doubt that private companies will provide a

113

better service than would the public sector;

(ii) there is no monopoly, so that there is open competition between providers of the service, to benefit customers in terms of price and quality; and

(iii) the good in question is not an essential good such as water, power or welfare benefits.[14]

Unfortunately, none of these conditions were satisfied in many of the privatisations. In fact, many of the services which were privatised had been nationally owned or owned by local authorities precisely because they were monopoly suppliers of essential services which might, if privately owned, exploit the customer.

In my view, the consequences of public-service privatisation should not be judged on a utilitarian basis but from an altogether different ethical perspective, one based on a duty of care for others, especially the vulnerable or needy. Customers who are not in any real sense customers, like benefits claimants, or who cannot help being customers, like water users, are vulnerable people because they are *powerless people*. When the public sector supplies such people with essential services the fact that the services are not run for profit protects them against exploitation; the public service ethos also safeguards their interests. If privatisation or 'marketisation' threaten the PSE, they reduce the protection for captive customers and particularly for the vulnerable. (This applies *a fortiori* to literally captive 'customers', the inmates of private prisons.) Reverting to the question of profits raised earlier, profits may not be unethical in principle, but it may be unethical to make a profit out of people's misfortunes, their vulnerability or life-essential needs. But that is too long and contentious a moral argument to embark on here.

Notes

1   R.H. Tawney, *Religion and the Rise of Capitalism* (Penguin, Harmondsworth, 1969), p.113.

2   M. Friedman, *Capitalism and Unfreedom*, 1962, quoted in E. Sternberg, *Just Business* (Little, Brown & Co., London, 1994), p.30.

3   Sternberg, *op.cit.*, p. 41.

4   J. S. Mill, *On Liberty* in Mill, *Utilitarianism*, ed. M. Warnock (Fontana, London, 1962), p. 243.

5   See J. Gray, *The Moral Foundations of Market Institutions*, Institute of Economic Affairs, London, 1992), especially the response by Raymond Plant. Also, A. Buchanan, *Ethics, Efficiency and the Market* (Clarendon Press, Oxford, 1985).

6   J. Jacobs, *Systems of Survival* (Hodder & Stoughton, London, 1992).

7   This contention is frequently repeated in his works: see C-H. de Saint-Simon, *Oeuvres de Claude-Henri de Saint-Simon* (Anthropos, Paris, 1966), vols. I-VI, *passim*.

8   These studies were carried out between 1995 and 1997. The material on which the following sub-sections are based is published in Henley Management College's Research Working Papers series (*HWP*). See B. Goodwin, 'Perceptions of Moral Responsibility and Ethical Questions: A Study of a Water Company', *HWP* 9511 (1995); 'Ethics and Responsibility in a London Borough (I)', *HWP* 9602 (1996); 'Ethics and Responsibility in a London Borough (II)' *HWP* 9603 (1996); 'Ethics and Responsibility in an Airline Company' *HWP* 9619 (1996); 'Ethics and Responsibility in a Government Agency' *HWP* 9717 (1997).

9   The Water study was my pilot study, and the issue of the PSE was raised by participants, not by me. In later studies I asked participants to comment on the PSE where appropriate.

10   R. Plant, 'Autonomy, social rights and distributive justice' in J. Gray, *op.cit.*, p.139.

11   *The Times*, 13.8.1997, p. 23.

12   C. Handy, 'What is a company for?', *Royal Society of Arts Journal*, March 1991, p.8.

13   Someone at the conference strongly disagreed that the demand for water was inelastic; I still think that 'relatively inelastic' is a reasonable description. I *must* use a certain minimum amount of water for living even if my supply is metered, but there is a 'natural' limit to the amount I will use if it is not metered and I am unlikely to use significantly greater amounts if the company reduces the cost of my (metered) supply. Demand inelasticity is,

evidently, a mixed blessing for the monopoly supplier!

14   You could say of air travel that nobody is *obliged* to travel by air but you
        could not say that of water or benefits.

7 Poverty and Social Exclusion

PHILLIP COLE

1. Introduction

This chapter examines the idea of social exclusion in relation to the poverty debate in the United Kingdom. Both the British Government and the European Union see poverty in terms of exclusion,[1] and social theorists on the left, particularly those attached to the Child Poverty Action Group, have characterised poverty as social exclusion since the 1980s.[2] The aim of this chapter is, partially, to attempt to clarify the concept - to explore how the idea of social exclusion can help us to understand poverty in the UK. This clarification takes place in part 2 of the chapter. However, the chapter also has a critical aim concerning how the idea has been used by the left in their critique of poverty. There are two levels to this criticism. The first problem is discussed in part 3 of the chapter, where I distinguish between two senses of social exclusion, a narrow and a wide sense. In the narrow sense, poverty excludes people from participating in specific activities and structures which are taken to constitute a 'normal' way of life within the society in question - for example sport and leisure activities. In the wide sense, people are excluded from active membership of their community, often described as being excluded from citizenship - the poor are only partial citizens of their own society. My concern here is that if these two senses of social exclusion become blurred, then the poverty boundary becomes blurred; the vast majority of people are only partial citizens, in that they are all, to some degree, excluded from some range of activities that constitutes full citizenship. In a sense, then, the narrow sense of social exclusion is more useful in a critique of poverty in Britain, in that it draws a much clearer poverty boundary. The wide sense of exclusion, with its appeal to the problematic notion of citizenship, should therefore be treated with some caution.

However, there is a much deeper critical concern, which I explore in part 4 of the chapter. Underlying the social exclusion thesis is the idea of participation - what people are excluded from, whether by poverty or other factors, is participation in the community, whether in the narrow sense of participation in specific activities or structures, or in the wide sense of participation as an active citizen. Inclusion therefore requires the empowerment to participate. The critical concern is that the notion of 'empowerment to participate' may not be as radical as it seems. Here we can distinguish between two senses of inclusion, a radical sense and a conservative sense. In the radical sense, people are included in that they are empowered to be genuinely autonomous members of the community, participating fully in its activities, structures, and decision-making procedures. In the conservative sense, people are not so much included, as *inserted* into the community: they are seen as people who have lost their allotted position in the social hierarchy through market misfortune, and are inserted into what is considered their appropriate social position. This can be seen as empowerment to participate, but the inserted person has no choice over the position they are allotted and therefore no choice over *how* they participate in the community. Something essential to the radical sense of inclusion is lost - the element of autonomous choice.

The left are, of course, arguing for the radical sense of inclusion, but the problem is that the focus on participation will not get them there. In order to arrive at the radical position, we have to look beyond participation as such, and think in terms of control - genuine inclusion would mean that people gain control over how they participate in the community. The problem for the poor in Britain is not so much that they are excluded from participation in society - they *are* participating within it. Rather, they have little or no control over *how* they participate; the majority of people, while they of course do not have complete control over how they participate, have a much greater degree of control, and therefore choice, than those in poverty.

2. Exclusion and Inclusion

The idea of social exclusion is used by many on the left as a counter to the idea of the underclass, which has been adopted by the New Right in Britain. While the notion of social exclusion has its most probable source in Continental Europe,[3] the idea of the underclass has been imported from the United States. The complex genesis of that idea and the statistical arguments for and against its relevance to Britain have been well documented elsewhere,[4] and I will not go over that material here. An important element of the New Right version of the underclass is moral condemnation of certain sections of the poor - certain groups are in poverty because of their behaviour.[5] However, the evidence seems to be that those who are more or less permanently in poverty in Britain are groups such as the physically disabled and the elderly,[6] who cannot be blamed for their 'failure' to escape poverty. Where some on the left do use the idea of the underclass, it is this kind of poverty they are trying to describe, and their use of the term lacks the moral condemnation which is essential to the New Right version.[7]

For the left, poverty is not a property the poor acquire through their behaviour, but a condition they find themselves in, created by processes over which they have no control. The poor are therefore not a separate class, they are ordinary members of the general population, sharing the same values, aspirations and ethics, and who are vulnerable to poverty because of the social, political and economic position they find themselves in. What the poor lack is not virtue, but the power to resist poverty. And so the idea of the underclass is rejected, and for Ruth Lister social exclusion is a preferable term: 'This is a more dynamic language which encourages a focus on the processes and institutions which create and maintain disadvantage rather than what can become a voyeuristic preoccupation with individual poor people and their behaviour.'[8]

However, the ideas of social exclusion and inclusion have to be explored in some detail. We can distinguish between two political senses of social exclusion and inclusion, a radical sense and a conservative sense. The radical understanding of exclusion holds that people are prevented from participating in their own community through poverty and other factors, and inclusion therefore means empowering people to be active members of that community. The conservative understanding sees exclusion as the loss of status in a social hierarchy, and inclusion as the insertion of people back into that social order. It is a conservative view in that it assumes the validity of a given social order with its hierarchy of status, and the concern over poverty is with its power to destabilize that order. Although it does see the poor as victims of social breakdown rather than as villains in need of discipline, the aim of social policy is to insert them into their appropriate place in the social order to ensure stability rather than increase their autonomy.

Bill Jordan sees the source of this conservative sense in what he calls the Continental mercantilist understanding of poverty, which he contrasts with the Anglo-Saxon liberal tradition.[9] The Anglo-Saxon liberal tradition saw poverty as a natural condition arising from the operation of the market, and the object of social policy was to ensure that the poor were not protected from such 'natural laws'. The Continental mercantilist tradition, in contrast,

119

saw the poor as victims of uncontrolled market forces, which threatened to break down the social order. 'In this tradition, the poor were more like sheep and cattle to be farmed (regulated and provided for as part of the creation and conservation of natural wealth) than wild animals to be tamed.'[10] If you like, their concern was for the lost sheep that had been separated from the flock by harsh conditions,[11] as opposed to the fear of the dog that has gone feral and is in need of discipline to tame it once more. The Anglo-Saxon tradition has its contemporary expression in the views of the New Right with the underclass thesis and its 'individual pathology.'[12] The Continental tradition still has its expression in Continental Europe, where social exclusion remains the focus of social policy. Jordan comments: 'The defining characteristics of European welfare states are that they both redistribute more resources and do so within systems of hierarchically ordered social-status groupings, whose relationships are regulated through the state. The poor are of concern because they have been relegated from these systems, by falling out of the labour market or the family, on which institutionalised social inclusion is based.'[13] And so 'social inclusion is increasingly pursued by compulsory measures for 'activating' or 'inserting' those who have fallen through the net.'[14]

Jordan draws on the work of Gosta Esping-Andersen,[15] who distinguishes between three models of the welfare state:

(1)   The liberal model, which assumes Jordan's Anglo-Saxon view of poverty: assistance is therefore means tested with modest social insurance and benefits aimed at only the very worst off. Here, 'the limits of welfare equal the marginal propensity to opt for welfare instead of work.'[16]

(2)   The corporatist-statist model, in which there is fairly strong entitlement to compulsory state insurance, but what is important is not promoting a work ethic, but preserving status differentials. This is Jordan's Continental mercantilist tradition.[17]

(3)   The social democratic model, based on universalism irrespective of contribution or performance. Esping-Andersen refers to this as the Beveridge approach.[18]

We have here three approaches to poverty: the liberal approach, which leads us to the idea of the undeserving underclass in need of discipline; and the conservative and left approaches, which both lead us to the ideas of inclusion and exclusion, but with very different understandings of what these

120

mean. The conservative approach sees the danger of poverty as the breakdown of social order, and social inclusion as the preservation of that order by *inserting* people into their appropriate place within it. The left approach sees the danger of poverty as the overwhelming of individuals by market forces and the destruction of their life-chances, and social inclusion as empowerment for the individual chooser. My primary critical concern is with the left approach, and that concern will occupy the rest of this essay.

3. Poverty and Citizenship

In the introduction to this paper I distinguished between a narrow and a wide sense of social exclusion, both of which can be found within left critiques of poverty. In the narrow sense, the poor are excluded from specific activities or structures, such as the transport system or leisure activity.[19] In the wide sense, people are excluded from citizenship as such,[20] with citizenship understood as active membership of the community. These two senses are, of course, linked in the critique of poverty, and the case being made is the very important one that poverty prevents people from being citizens in their own society. However, there is a danger attached to the wide sense of social exclusion with its appeal to the idea of citizenship.

Ruth Lister distinguishes between two conceptions of citizenship: firstly, citizenship expressed as active membership of society; and secondly, citizenship as a critical vision of that society.[21] It is the first of these senses of citizenship that is at issue when Peter Golding talks of 'the right to full and adequately supported membership of the community, of citizenship...',[22] and Ruth Lister says: '...membership of a community is understood in terms of participation in that community. This participation is an expression both of the formal political, legal and social rights and duties of citizenship, and of the social and economic conditions under which they are exercised.'[23] And it is the second of them that is at stake when Ruth Lister says: '...citizenship is regarded as an ideal, a goal which is once again acting as an inspiration to those who are trying to construct an alternative vision of society.'[24]

The distinction being made, then, is between citizenship as we find it in Britain, the activities that are taken to constitute active membership of society as it exists; and citizenship as a critical vision of that society, bringing with it the possibility of a radically participatory community, with extensive opportunities for democratic citizenship for all. The difficulty with this second, much more radical, vision of citizenship, is that we are *all* excluded from *that* political community. Or to put it another way, if poverty excludes people from participating as active members of a political community of equal citizens, then the poor in Britain are being excluded from a community that does not exist; even if they were not economically poor, they would not be full members of a community of equal and active citizens, because such a political community is not in place. But why should this be a difficulty for the left critique of poverty? Lister is quite clear that this conception of citizenship is an ideal, an alternative vision of society. The problem is that such an approach blurs the divisions in society, and most importantly blurs the poverty line: the poor are no more excluded from this conception of citizenship than the vast majority of the population.

It could be replied that as long as we are clear that this radical view of citizenship is a critical vision no confusion should arise. We still have the former view of citizenship, active membership of society as we find it, and this can play a useful role in the critique of poverty. However, this is debatable. The point of this approach is that 'poverty is most comprehensively understood as a condition of partial citizenship.'[25] Poverty prevents people from participating in a range of activities taken to constitute active membership of society. However, there is a danger that when we attempt to spell out what fully active membership consists of, we are once more describing a critical vision, rather than a condition that many people in Britain actually enjoy - partial citizenship can be caused by many factors other than poverty, and is, I would argue, a condition that afflicts a large part of the population. The poverty line is, again, in danger of being blurred.

The narrow conception of social exclusion can be made sense of without appeal to the rhetoric of citizenship. John Scott describes poverty as: '...a lack of the economic resources that are necessary for the enjoyment of a basic standard of living, however this is seen in the particular society in question. The poor are those who are 'deprived' of the conditions necessary for an adequate life in the society in which they live.'[26] Of course, there are going to be difficulties and complexities in spelling out what counts as an 'adequate' life, and I am not going to attempt to define one here. However, I do believe these difficulties are not at the same level as those involved in attempting to define what constitutes citizenship. It could be replied that such an approach is too cautious, and that the idea of citizenship provides a radical cutting edge to the critique of poverty, missing if we focus only on what constitutes an 'adequate' life. However, the point is that the critical edge provided by the radical conception of citizenship reveals the inadequacy of

122

the position the vast majority of the population suffer, in terms of political power and influence. The adequate life approach allows us to focus on the specific problems faced by the poor in Britain, and has the potential to provide a clear poverty boundary. And so I do believe that the rhetoric of citizenship has to be treated with some caution in the left critique of poverty.

There is, however, a deeper problem with the left critique of poverty in terms of social exclusion, and that is the focus upon exclusion from participation. It is this problem that I discuss in the rest of the chapter.

4. Poverty and Power

Ruth Lister notes that the debate over the underclass and social exclusion rests on an agency/structure contrast, with the underclass approach identifying individual agency as the cause of (some) poverty and the social exclusion approach identifying social structures.[27] But this reveals a danger for the left, which Lister notes: that the emphasis on structure over agency can lead to a view of the poor as helpless and passive victims of poverty. There needs to be a balance between focusing on structural constraints, and recognising that the poor are 'also agents or actors in their own lives.'[28] The danger is that the poverty debate can become framed by a distinction between active villains and passive victims: if the poor are active villains they must be policed and disciplined; if they are passive victims they must be 'cared for' - and so a welfare system emerges which is a mixture of disciplinary policies and patronising social services.

The left attempt to transcend this dichotomy by emphasising the need to empower people to participate in society, but this in itself may not be enough: participation in itself is not the key to inclusion. Saul Becker develops the idea of social exclusion by examining the disability movement.[29] If the active villain/passive victim dichotomy frames the debate, then the disabled fall on the 'passive victim' side of the divide, and so are likely to be subjected to patronising and disempowering forms of care. To break out of this oppressive framework the key idea is not care, but control - what matters is the degree of control the disabled have over their own activities, and the share of control they have over the social institutions that affect them. Becker points out that the ultimate expression of social exclusion is 'segregation and control in institutions,'[30] something both the disabled and the poor have been subjected to. But, argues Becker, rather than simply move beyond institutionalisation to a model of 'care in the community', we have to put in place a framework which ensures, firstly, that cash benefits are set at a level which enables social participation and control, and secondly, that personal social services are such that they empower and enable people to take control over their lives.

This has been recognised by the left in their critique of poverty. Peter Golding comments: 'Poverty excludes, and not least it excludes from power and influence.'[31] And this does seem central to the radical social exclusion thesis, that the poor are excluded from power, rather than merely from participation. However, we have to keep in mind that we do not want to say that the poor are being excluded from a radically democratic system of power, because such a system is not in place - if we are going to focus on the poverty divide, then we need to be clear what sort of power the poor are excluded from.

Here again, the key idea is control. The idea of control takes us further than the idea of participation alone, once we recognise that one can participate in an activity in a way which is itself disempowering - one can be included in an activity, but in a way that still excludes one from any control over it. Genuine inclusion will mean, not only participation in an activity or institution, but some degree of control over the form of that participation, and therefore over that activity or institution. From the point of view of disability, this means, for example, looking beyond ramps to get people confined to wheelchairs into the workplace, without any regard for the quality of work that they have to undertake once they are 'included' in the workforce. The idea of control is therefore crucial, if empowering people to participate is going to move beyond mere *insertion*, and be genuinely inclusive.

The idea of control is complex,[32] but for the purposes of this discussion, one has control over an activity or institution if one determines the form of that activity or institution and/or its outcomes. Control is not merely the *capacity* to determine these, it is the actual determination of them. One can possess *power* in the sense of having the capacity to determine outcomes, without having to exercise that capacity - but to possess control, the outcomes have to be actually determined; power does not need to be exercised, but control does. Control, then, is power successfully exercised. This means there are two ways in which one can fail to have control over an activity or institution: firstly, one has the power to control it but does not exercise that power for whatever reason; or second, one lacks the power to control it. The poor lack control in the second sense.

Power is, of course, an extremely complex concept, and my discussion of it here is necessarily compressed. Jeanne Neath and Kay

Schriner[33] distinguish between three forms of power:[34]

(1)   personal power - 'the power of the individual to influence her environment'; or 'the ability or potential of the individual to act to obtain desired consequences'.
(2)   power over - 'hierarchical, authoritarian social power...'; or 'a form of social power based in domination and characterised by hierarchy and inequality in relationships'.
(3)   power with - 'egalitarian social power, the power to act together as equal partners'; or 'a form of social power where people come together as equals'.[35]

This reveals the limitations of an approach based upon empowerment to participate, as Neath and Schriner complain that the focus of empowerment policies for the disabled has been the first kind of power.[36] While this has obvious benefits, it remains a limited strategy given the way power is structured in society: if social power is overwhelmingly of type (2), then any power of type (1) that is created is likely to be easily overwhelmed. This is especially problematic when it comes to empowering the disabled through employment because the workplace is predominantly a power structure of type (2). 'All workers except those at the very top of a workplace hierarchy also experience being on the underside of *power over* relationships.'[37] Again, this is especially problematic for the disabled, because: 'Unfortunately, the vast majority of workers with severe disabilities have low status jobs.'[38] The solution that Neath and Schriner explore is the construction of workplaces around type (3) power.

Control can obviously be the actualisation of all three power types: one can have personal control over one's activities; control over other people's activities; and control shared with other people over institutions. Whichever kind of control is seen as most progressive, the fact is that the poor are excluded from all of them. More importantly, there are three ways in which this lack of control is expressed:

(1)   People may lack the power to gain access to an activity or institution at all. If we take the example of access to transport, they may not be able to afford to use either private or public transport. This is the most obvious sense of exclusion, and is, I suspect, what it is often taken to mean. However, it is too limited, in that there are two other

important forms in which exclusion can be expressed.

(2)   Where people *do* participate in activities and institutions, they may lack control over that participation - they are participating in society, but they have little or no control over how they participate. Again, if we take the example of transport, they may be able to afford access to public transport, but this places severe limits upon their control over their movement in that they are restricted to whatever timetable the transport system operates by. A person with private transport has a much greater capacity to control their movement, and can normally determine to be in a particular place at a specific time. A person dependent on public transport has far less control, and can only be in a particular place if the public transport system services that place, and at whatever time the system allows. This is especially problematic where public transport systems are rare, such as in rural areas. This demonstrates how someone is participating in an activity - here, travel activity - and yet have little control over *how* they participate.

(3)   A person can have control over how they participate in an activity, but the space in which they have such control is small - they *can* determine the form and outcomes of the activity, but these are very narrowly confined. Using transport as the example again, a person may have complete control over their movement despite having no access to private transport and restricted access to public transport, in that they can travel under their own power, for example by walking. However, the physical space within which they can exercise this control is very limited - it remains the space they can cover in a reasonable time on foot.

This schema can be applied to many such activities, and shows that the fact that one can participate in an activity or institution is not enough to show that one has any degree of power or influence over that activity; or where one does have power or influence over it, that power can only be effective in a very limited space. Social exclusion is therefore highly complex and can have many dimensions.

5. Conclusion

While poverty can be understood as a deprivation of economic resources, social exclusion cannot - rather, it is deprivation of power, and this moves us beyond an exclusive focus on economic and material condition in that people can lack power, and therefore be socially excluded, for many different reasons. It is important to recognise that social exclusion can be experienced not only in relation to poverty and disablement, but also in relation to racism, sexism, homophobia and other forms of exclusion from power and influence.[39] Equally, it is important to note that poverty has dimensions other than social exclusion: the United Nations identifies four measures of poverty: life expectancy, deprivation in knowledge, deprivation in income, and social exclusion.[40] What, then, is the specific connection between poverty and social exclusion?

For Saul Becker, social exclusion is connected with the relative conception of poverty. Absolute poverty is linked with subsistence: 'poverty occurs only when and where people have insufficient resources to provide the minimum necessary to sustain life'.[41] Relative poverty, however, is not simply inequality: '...poverty has to be understood as a dynamic concept, and measured in relation to the living standards which are generally accepted in the society, and at the time, in question.'[42] Peter Townsend, in developing the notion of relative poverty, has argued that as people descend the income scale, their participation 'in the community's style of living' reduces.[43] What distinguishes relative poverty from inequality is that there is a threshold at which the impact upon people's control is catastrophic: '...a threshold of income which really does have an effect in terms of mortality, of the isolation of people, their withdrawal from citizenship roles, family roles and so on...'[44] And so Becker concludes: 'Today, the concept of poverty, in its relative sense, centres on the notion of exclusion from social participation.'[45]

The picture becomes clearer if we distinguish between two kinds of exclusion, economic and social. Economic exclusion is to be excluded from control over economic resources, while social exclusion is to be excluded from control over society and one's place within it. One point to note here is that one can be economically excluded and not be classed below the poverty line - the patriarchal nuclear family normally places women in a position of economic exclusion, in that they have little or no control over economic resources, but they are not necessarily classed as being in poverty. The problem of poverty is primarily to do with economic exclusion, but it is not simply a problem of lack of control over economic resources: rather, there is a level of economic deprivation which causes social exclusion, a level at which, as Townsend has argued, people have little choice but to withdraw from social activity. The economic threshold which marks this event is the point at which we can say people are in relative poverty, and therefore constitutes the poverty boundary. And so social exclusion becomes a necessary component of relative poverty.

What is more important here is to clarify what social exclusion means in this context. I have argued that the poor are not excluded from participation as such, although their poverty may indeed exclude them from *any* participation in particular activities in some cases. Rather, they are excluded from control over the extent to which they participate in activities and institutions, and the form their participation takes. Therefore empowerment to participate is not sufficient from a radical point of view, and a welfare system that focuses on inclusion in this sense alone is in danger of becoming a system of insertion rather than genuine inclusion. This is especially problematic in the area of work - the welfare system may empower people to work, and ensure their participation in the labour market, but may give them little or no control over the work they do. It is here that we see exclusion, in all its forms, in the context of the market system. As Esping-Anderson argues,[46] under the capitalist market system people are commodifed - their welfare depends entirely on access to the cash nexus through the sale of their labour power. Therefore people are excluded to the extent that they have limited or no labour power that can be sold in that market, due to social attitudes to physical disability, or patriarchy in the home, for example. However, inserting them into the labour market does *not* de-commodify them from the demands of the market - it is simply to *meet* those demands. And so a radical position would aim at a system of empowerment *and* emancipation - a system than empowers people to participate, but at the same time emancipates them from restrictions upon their autonomy when it comes to choosing how to participate; it would have to liberate people from the demands of market forces. Unless we recognise that what people are socially excluded from is power over participation, rather than merely opportunity to participate, we will lose that essential element of the radical attack upon poverty.

Notes

1   Among the first acts of the newly elected Labour government was the setting up of a Social Exclusion Unit, which is due to start reporting in 1998. The European Union also sees poverty as, to some extent, connected to social exclusion. The EU's fourth poverty programme aims to 'combat exclusion

and promote solidarity' (House of Lords Select Committee on the European Communities, *The Poverty Programme* (HMSO, London 1994), p.7). And: 'The poor shall be taken to mean persons, families and groups of persons whose resources (material, cultural and social) are so limited as to exclude them from the minimum acceptable way of life in the member states in which they live.' From Golding, P., 'Public Attitudes to Social Exclusion: Some Problems of Measurement and Analysis', in Room, G., ed., *Beyond the Threshold: the Measurement and Analysis of Social Exclusion* (Bristol, Polity Press, 1995), p.213.

2 See Ruth Lister, *The Exclusive Society: Citizenship and the Poor* (London, Child Poverty Action Group, 1990), Peter Golding, ed., *Excluding the Poor* (London, Child Poverty, Action Group, 1986) and Alan Walker and Carol Walker, eds., *Britain Divided: the Growth of Social Exclusion in the 1980s and 1990s* (London, Child Poverty Action Group, 1997).

3 See Bill Jordan, *A Theory of Poverty and Social Exclusion* (London, Polity Press 1996), pp.3-4.

4 See Lister, *The Exclusive Society*, pp.24-26; Ruth Lister, ed., *Charles Murray and the Underclass: the Developing Debate* (Institute of Economic Affairs, London, 1996); and John Scott, *Poverty and Wealth: Citizenship, Deprivation and Privilege* (Longman, London and New York, 1994), pp.161-174.

5 For example, David Green comments that the underclass constitutes those amongst the poor 'distinguished by their undesirable behaviour, including drug-taking, crime, illegitimacy, failure to hold down a job, truancy from school and casual violence'; in Lister ed., *Charles Murray and the Underclass*, p. 19.

6 See Scott, *Poverty and Wealth*, p.168.

7 See Frank Field, 'Britain's Underclass: Countering the Growth', in Lister, ed., *Charles Murray and the Underclass*.

8 Lister, ed., *Charles Murray and the Underclass*, Introduction, p.11.

9 Jordan, op. cit. pp.3-4.

10 Jordan, op. cit. p.4.

11 But with Thrasymachus' understanding of the aims of the shepherd, rather

129

than that of Socrates. See Plato's *Republic*, 345c-e, p.87 (Penguin Books, Harmondsworth, 1979).

12   Jordan, op. cit. p.3.

13   Jordan, op. cit. p.3.

14   Jordan, op. cit. p.3.

15   Gosta Esping-Andersen, *The Three Worlds of Welfare Capitalism* (Cambridge, Polity Press, 1990).

16   Esping-Andersen, ibid. p.26, and see p.22.

17   Esping-Andersen, ibid. p.22 and p.27.

18   Esping-Andersen, ibid. pp.22-23 and p.28.

19   For this approach, see Golding, ed., *Excluding the Poor*.

20   For this approach, see Lister, *The Exclusive Society*.

21   Lister, *The Exclusive Society*, p.2.

22   Lister, *The Exclusive Society*, Peter Golding, Foreword, p.vii.

23   Lister, ibid. p.2.

24   Lister, ibid. p.2.

25   Golding, ed., *Excluding the Poor*, p.xi.

26   Scott, *Poverty and Wealth*, p.17.

27   Lister, *Charles Murray and the Underclass*, pp.11-12.

28   Lister, ibid. p.12.

29   Saul Becker, *Responding to Poverty: The Politics of Cash and Care* (London and New York, Longman, 1997), pp.55-56.

30   Becker, ibid. p.56.

31   Golding, ed., *Excluding the Poor*, p.x.

32   And a curiously underdeveloped one - few of the many discussions of poverty analyse the idea of control in any depth.

33   Jeanne Neath and Kay Schriner, 'Power to People with Disabilities: Empowerment Issues in Employment Programming', *Disability and Society* Volume 13 Number 2, April 1998, pp.217-228. They draw on the work of S. Kreisberg, *Transforming Power: Domination, Empowerment and Education* (Albany, State University of New York, 1992).

34   Neath and Schriner, ibid. p.218.

35   Neath and Schriner, ibid. p.219.

36   Neath and Schriner, ibid. p.217.

37   Neath and Schriner, ibid. p.220.

38   Neath and Schriner, ibid. p.220.

39   And, of course, these different experiences of social exclusion can interact, such that the way in which women, for example, experience poverty is distinctive.

40   See *The Guardian* newspaper, Wednesday 9th September 1998, p.2: 'Britain's Poor Are Worse Off Than Ever, Says UN'.

41   Becker, *Responding to Poverty*, p.21.

42   Becker, ibid. p.24.

43   Becker, ibid. p.24.

44   See Becker, ibid. pp.24-25.

45   Becker, ibid. p.25.

46   Esping-Andersen, *The Three Worlds of Welfare Capitalism*, pp.21-23.

8 Social Justice and Process versus End-state Conceptions of Competition

DAVID MERRILL

Contemporary theories of justice tend to overlook the workings of the market as an ethical issue. Either they claim that market relations are inherently unjust, as some Marxists do, or concern themselves with factors that fall outside the actual procedures of the economy. The latter may seek to remedy the distribution of income that the economy produces, as basic income theories do, or intervene upon the character of the agencies taking part in economic life. It may be proposed that the initial assets of the individual about to enter the economy be adjusted, or the structure of firms may be required to take a certain shape, as recommended in theories of market socialism. Yet, in actual economic life, the procedures of the economy are not overlooked, for they do not take care of themselves. Economic processes cannot be taken as a given, but require continual intervention. Furthermore, because the economy is not something fixed, there is the suggestion that the public regulation of and intervention in the market is an ethical matter. Consequently, to assume the economy as a given both violates the sense of how economies actually work and overlooks what should be a major area of ethical deliberation.

How do contemporary theories overlook what is here proposed as an essential feature of economic life, both as empirically observed and as morally and ethically conceived? It is the main task of this chapter to show that in the case of John Rawls's *A Theory of Justice*,[1] the oversight is sustained, at least in part, through making certain assumption regarding the economy. Specifically, the inquiry here concerns Rawls's reasoned case for his first principles of social justice (as opposed to the justification based on the social contract, choice procedures of the original position,) and claims that there Rawls takes it as given that the economy is perfectly competitive. It is true that he makes the distinction between his view of the economy used in the development of his principles of social justice and his view of the actual economy that the authorities, who seek to implement his principles, will face. Only the former is perfectly competitive. But it is the former view that is of greater consequence for it is that one which provides the determining context for his principles of justice.

Consequently, when the economic assumptions are questioned, his conclusions regarding the principles of justice are also put in doubt. As the paper will show, to criticize the assumption of competitive markets, as Rawls uses the expression, is to criticize, in particular, the primary principle in his theory of social justice, the difference principle. For it will be argued that the difference principle is intrinsically linked to this assumption of the perfectly competitive market. The alternative to Rawls's view of the economy cast in terms of the end-state equilibriums of perfect competition, is the notion of market competition as a process which reaches no final equilibrium.[2] Such a different context calls for different principles of justice which will be briefly addressed at the end. It will be suggested that a way ahead can be made by not assuming that the market economy takes any particular fixed shape, and by extending the idea of equal opportunity so that it can address this new context.

1

Rawls's argument for the difference principle examined here is that which Brian Barry refers to as based on the notion of justice as impartiality.[3] This is the justification Rawls presents in his second chapter. There, Rawls begins his justification of his difference principle by making a general statement about his two principles of justice. The first principle claims that, 'each person is to have an equal right to the most extensive basic liberty compatible with a similar liberty for others.' His second principle, which is the one relevant to the inquiry here, states that 'social and economic inequalities are to be arranged so that they are both (a) reasonably expected to be to everyone's advantage, and (b) attached to positions and offices open to all' (60). Both these principles are to apply to the basic structure of society and both principles concern distributive issues (60-61).

The items whose distribution is the concern of the theory of justice are those things that every rational man is presumed to want, or what Rawls calls primary goods. Chief among these are right and liberties, powers and opportunities, income and wealth. With respect to the second principle, the aim of Rawls's theory is to establish rules for that part of the basic structure of society which determines the distribution of income and wealth and which pertains to the designs of the organizations in which positions are ranked hierarchically in terms of authority and responsibility. The principle will require of such institutions not that income and wealth be evenly distributed but that any inequalities will be to everyone's advantage and that positions must be accessible to all (62).

Rawls's theory also requires that the second part, (b), of this principle, that having to with the openness of positions is lexically prior to the first part (a), concerning distribution. In other words, the question of the just distribution of income and wealth can only be raised after the condition concerning the openness of positions has been satisfied (61). Finally, as these principles have to do with the design of institutions, the theory's treatment will have to do with the expectations of individuals. Determining a certain design for an institution does not in itself determine the specific economic outcome for an individual but rather the likelihood of certain outcomes. 'Neither principle applies to distributions of particular goods to particular individuals who may be identified by their proper names' (64).

The development of this general account of the second principle to something more specific, comes through Rawls's assertion that each clause, (a) and (b), has two interpretations, which when combined appropriately advance the theory. For (a), the expression, 'to everyone's advantage', can be interpreted to mean either the principle of efficiency or Rawls's difference principle. Clause (b), the notion of positions equally open, can signify either equality as careers open to talents or equality as equality of fair opportunity. Through the appropriate combination of these two pairs of interpretations, Rawls provides both a justification and a specification of his difference principle. The process of combination leads to three stages in the development of his theory. While the first two do constitute a positive development of the theory of justice they are ultimately inadequate, and thus require the theory's continual development until it reaches the last stage (65-66).

The first step is made in combining the first interpretations of each of the two parts of Rawls's principle of social justice. When the principle of efficiency is combined with the notion of equality as careers open to talents, the result is a regime Rawls calls the system of natural liberty. In this regime the basic structures of society conform to the efficiency principle and positions in society are available on the basis of careers open to talents. Yet these two principles are not sufficient to specify the main features of the society of natural liberty. He must introduce the economy to provide the context for his principles of justice. It is in the economy that his principles get realized. Yet, though essential, the economy comes into the theory only as an assumption.[4] Specifically, it is assumed that the economy is 'roughly a free market system, although the means of production may or may not be privately owned' (66).

Yet, it is worth pausing to ask, what are the grounds for the certainty that the economy will satisfy the criterion of efficiency. The society will be one where careers are open to talents because it will be the duty of a public authority to guarantee it. But what ensures that the economy will meet the proposed criteria? The answer implicit in Rawls is rooted in his use of the principle of efficiency. For, while there will be more supportive evidence later in the text, it is possible to surmise already, that in his use of the principle of efficiency, Rawls is indicating that by market economy he means what economists call a perfectly competitive economy.

Rawls claims that the basic structure of society will operate in conformity to the principle of efficiency, or what is the same thing, the principle of Pareto optimality (66). He gives a definition of the principle.

> The principle holds that a configuration is efficient whenever it is impossible to change it so as to make some persons (at least one) better off without at the same time making other persons (at least one) worse off. Thus a distribution of a stock of commodities among certain individuals is efficient if there exists no redistribution of these goods that improves the circumstances of at least one of these individuals without another being disadvantaged (67).

Rawls does not explain, though, what his commitment to the principle of efficiency means at this point regarding the nature of the economy he has assumed. The consequences must be inferred.

If the economy is producing results that are Pareto optimal, then it will require a particular structure of a complexity not suggested by the passage quoted above. Specifically, the economy will be efficient if and only if it is perfectly competitive. The connection between perfect competition and efficiency or Pareto optimality is summed up in what are called the 'fundamental theorems' of welfare economics. These theorems state, according to Mark Blaug, 'not only that a long-run perfectly competitive equilibrium will yield an optimum allocation of resources, always with respect to the proviso that the distribution of income is given, but also that every optimum allocation of resources is a long-run perfectly competitive equilibrium'.[5] Thus, though Rawls does not say that his free market is a perfectly competitive one, it appears to be the necessary consequence of his criterion of social efficiency.

For an explanation of what constitutes perfectly competitive equilibrium, it is helpful to turn to an account which is, admittedly, highly critical, by Joan Robinson.

> Equilibrium has been defined in these terms: 'Prices and input-output combinations are said to be equilibrium prices and input-output combinations if, when they rule, no economic agent has any inducement to change his method of production, and no input is in excess demand.'
>
> This entails that everyone knows exactly and in full detail what consequences would follow any action that he may take. (Indeed, the condition for reaching equilibrium is often stated to be 'perfect foresight'.) It rules out the holding of stock or money balances for contingencies, and it rules out any plans, say, for business investment or household saving, with consequences spread over future time in which circumstances are liable to change.
>
> There is another curious feature of the concept. Equilibrium is described as 'the end of an economic process'; the story is usually told of a group of individuals each with an 'endowment' of ready-made goods or of productive capacity of some specific kind. By trading and retrading in a market, each ends up with a selection of goods that he prefers to those that he started with. If we interpret this as a historical process, it implies that, in the period of past time leading to 'today', equilibrium was not established. Why are conditions that led to a non-equilibrium position 'today' not going to be present in the future?...
>
> Some theorists, even among those who reject general equilibrium as useless, praise its logical elegance and completeness. A system of simultaneous equations need not specify any date nor does its solution involve history. But if any proposition drawn from it is applied to an economy inhabited by human beings, it immediately becomes self-contradictory. Human life does not exist outside history and no one has correct foresight of his own future behaviour, let alone of the behaviour of all the other individuals which will impinge upon his. I do not think it is right to praise the logical elegance of a system which becomes self-contradictory when it is applied to the question that it was designed to answer.[6]

No effort will made here to set out in any further detail an explanation of what constitutes perfect competition. Nor will the idea be fully examined whether the economics of perfect competition has the deficiencies Robinson identifies, or whether theories of perfectly competitive equilibrium can be modified to overcome the deficiencies its critics identify. Rather than pursuing further elaboration of this economic theory, the inquiry here will stick with how the economy is being used in Rawls. The critique of Rawls can be made separately from proving what constitutes perfect competition, whether Rawls assumes it and what influence that specific assumption makes on his theory. The point to be stressed is that the orientation to equilibrium end-states inherent in theories of the perfectly competitive economy is also characteristic of Rawls. Whether Rawls does assume in some precise sense that the economy is perfectly competitive is secondary. Taking this course makes sense, in part because Rawls does not detail what sort of economy he has in mind. Without further ado, Rawls simply takes it as given that economic procedures, at this point in his theory, are essentially movements from initial states to end-states. The intermediary stages pose no concerns. The economy is not viewed as a continually changing process.

To understand better this distinction between views of the market economy in terms of end-state equilibriums and as an ongoing process, it is helpful again to turn to Blaug for his development of the distinction. While his comments on this distinction come in his critique of general equilibrium theory, they have a significance independent of the specifics of perfect competition.

> ...one of the deepest divides in the history of economics...[is] between the notion of competition as an *end-state* of rest in the rivalry between buyers and sellers and competition as a *process* of rivalry that may or may not terminate in an end-state. In the end-state conception of competition, the focus of attention is on the nature of the equilibrium state in which the contest between market traders is finally resolved; if there is recognition of change at all, it is change in the sense of a new stationary equilibrium of endogenous variables defined in terms of a different set of exogenous variables; but comparative statics is still an end-state conception of competition. However, in the process conception of competition, it is not the existence of equilibrium that is in the foreground of analysis but rather the stability of that equilibrium state. How do markets adjust when one equilibrium is displaced by another and at what speed will these markets converge to a new equilibrium...
>
> The replacement of the process conception of competition by an end-state conception, which was finalised by 1933 or thereabouts, drained the idea of competition of all behavioural content, so that even price competition, the very essence of the competitive process for Smith, Ricardo and Mill, now had to be labelled and analysed as 'imperfect' or 'monopolistic' competition. Indeed, every act of rivalry on the part of a business was now taken as evidence of some degree of monopoly power and

hence a departure from perfect competition. By an extraordinary transformation of ideas, the theory of perfect competition had finally become a description of a state of competition that was literally impossible and excluded everything that had ever been thought of as competitive behaviour. The result was an acute disjunction between the economists' case for competition and the layman's case. For the economist, competition was good because when it was perfect, it was Pareto-optimal. For the lay-man, competition was good because it maximised the technical dynamism of an economy and produced an ever-growing volume of goods at the lowest possible prices and if this kind of competitive system required big business, it mattered not. These are defences so different in kind as not to inhabit the same universe.[7]

Blaug's warnings about conceiving the economy in terms of end-states, points to the possibility that Rawls's theory, in overlooking the procedures by which economic fortunes are established, may equally be overlooking essential components in the determination of the just society. If this is the case then the charge of a fundamental lack of realism that Blaug makes against certain economic theories will apply also to Rawls's theory of justice. In other words, the sort of inadequacies to be found in general equilibrium theory may also appear in analogous form in Rawls's ethical theory. Both ignore the ever shifting and changing nature of actual economic life because both conceive economic relations in terms of the move from an initial position to a timeless equilibrium.

If it is accepted that Robinson and Blaug are right in their claims about the damaging lack of reality to end-state theories of economic competition, then the following suggestion arises. The end-state notions of economic competition, such as found in Rawls, arise more from a commitment to the principle of efficiency as a key tool in theory building, rather than a commitment to find abstract but plausible notions of the economy. But whatever the motivation behind the economic assumptions there is more at stake than empirical plausibility. There is a moral and ethical issue at stake. This is not a point made by Robinson and Blaug, but one appropriate to this examination of social justice. This is that notions of competitive markets, cast in terms of end-state equilibriums, exclude a notion of the individual (and other economic agents) as both free and acting through time with a multitude of other equally free individuals (and other economic agents). Not only does the perfect competition model only incorporate very narrow and contrived kinds of economic behaviour, the individual's economic freedom is also curtailed by the lack of recognition that the individual can

138

change course throughout an economic life. When this essential dimension of freedom is incorporated into the model of the economy, then it is impossible to portray the economy as having all its markets cleared, as does perfect competition theory. Rather, with individuals acting freely and in time, then one should expect that markets will not clear. A morally or ethically accurate portrayal of the market should be one where because of the component of freedom, there will be a continual disequilibrium of supply and demand in all markets and, as well, in market-wide terms.

2

Given these comments on end-state notions of economic equilibrium, the ramifications for Rawls's principles of justice need now to be fully set out. It is therefore necessary to return to the development of his theory. In Rawls's discussion of the principle of efficiency, he readily admits to the inadequacy of such a principle alone to govern society. The principle of efficiency permits any number of extreme imbalances in the distribution of society's benefits and burdens. This possibility of a multitude of equally valid points, and the opposition of many of them to conventional intuitions of just social distributions, points up the limitations of the principle of efficiency (71). However, Rawls does not abandon the principle, but rather proposes further principles that can check the invalid aspects. In other words, the suggestion is that for Rawls, while the principle of efficiency may be a necessary condition of the just society, it is not a sufficient condition. Thus the principle of equality as careers open to talents is introduced to meet deficiencies identified within the principle of efficiency.

The principle of careers open to talents entails a formal equality of opportunity. Rawls refers to this having as 'at least the same legal rights of access to all advantaged social positions' (72). Though he does not say so, one can imagine by this that discrimination in the area of employment based on race, sex, age, creed and so on, is prohibited, and that other types of fair employment practices must be incorporated into employment law. Rawls then asks whether the society of natural liberty will do as an account of social justice. He begins his answer by revealing more of his thoughts on the nature of the economy upon which his principles of justice are to be applied. As will be seen, they remain consistent with discussion above of end-state notions of economic equilibrium.

The essential point Rawls wants to establish is that in his view, the economy in his theory is one where differences in distributional outcomes are determined by differences in the distribution of initial assets.

Let us suppose that we know from economic theory that under the standard assumptions defining a competitive market economy, income and wealth will be distributed in an efficient way, and that the particular efficient distribution which results in any period of time is determined by the initial distribution of assets, that is, by the initial distribution of income and wealth, and of natural talents and abilities. With each initial distribution, a definite efficient outcome is arrived at. Thus it turns out that if we are to accept the outcome as just, and not merely efficient, we must accept the basis upon which over time the initial distribution of assets is determined (72).

Given that he sees that the actual workings of the economy make no contribution to differentials in economic outcomes, it seems clear that for all intents and purposes, in using the expression, 'competitive market economy', his position remains consistent with end-state notions of economic theory discussed above. Setting aside the details of perfect competition theory, this assumption that the actual workings of the economy make no independent contribution of their own to economic outcomes seems, to repeat, to violate an important dimension of realism and deny an essential freedom to economic man and woman.

By limiting himself to this notion of the economy, Rawls radically limits the factors which affect any one individual's economic outcomes. The individual will never face a situation of actual over or undersupply of labour, commodities, means of production, land and so on, either in general economy wide terms or in terms of specific industries, localities or occupations. None of these regular factors of actual economic life, or of economic life conceived as an ethical realm of free conduct, will require the attention of his principles of justice. The assumption of the competitive market economy has overcome such difficulties.

Of course, these inadequacies are not the ones upon which Rawls focuses. Instead, Rawls points out that the regime of natural liberty permits natural and social contingencies to influence the initial distribution of assets and so the economy's distribution of income and wealth. Intuition suggests that the influence of contingent natural and social factors over the distribution of initial assets is morally arbitrary (72). Perhaps Rawls believes that the intuition in question concerns the idea that as these factors are not subject to the free will, they should have no place in determining what is the just social distribution. It is necessary to introduce further constraints on the operation of the economy that can neutralize these morally arbitrary factors. The principle Rawls introduces to address these deficiencies is the principle of fair equality of opportunity. This, combined with the strictures of the system of natural liberty, produces the regime of what Rawls calls liberal equality.

3

The aim of liberal equality is to nullify the influence of social factors in the distribution of initial assets. When this is accomplished the result should be that, given that there will be variety in the distribution of the natural assets of talent and ability, 'those who are at the same level of talent and ability, and have the same willingness to use them, should have the same prospects of success regardless of their initial place in the social system, that is, irrespective of the income class into which they are born' (73). The measures required to implement liberal equality will entail further interventions into the basic structure of the social system. The policies that Rawls highlights call for the prevention of excessive accumulation of property and wealth, and the regulation of the school system so that it neutralises the significance of class (73). Yet, it is obvious, as Rawls acknowledges, that these measures only tackle one of the two sources of moral arbitrariness left unaddressed by the prior system of natural liberty. The constraints placed upon society by the principle of fair opportunity do nothing about the economic differentials due to the morally arbitrary factor of differentials in the initial natural assets of talent and ability.

Furthermore, it can be expected that efforts around the regulation of the school system and the prevention of excessive accumulation of wealth and property will not nullify all the benefits an advantaged social background may bring to an individual. Rawls recognises that significant advantages of a privileged social position are transmitted, not only through income and capital differentials, or even schooling, but through the family. Differences in what might be called the cultures of families can result in differences in economic outcomes. Yet, given society's respect for the traditions of family life, it is unlikely that there are public measures that would be both widely acceptable and sufficiently effective in transforming family life to overcome these unfair advantages that families transmit (74).

Rawls concludes that social and economic regulation can go only so far, and that there are certain morally arbitrary factors, which cannot be excluded from the basket of initial assets. Equality of opportunity can address only a part of the social injustices that exist. Accordingly, it is necessary to add a further principle to the collection of social norms which make up liberal equality. This further principle is Rawls's famous difference principle, the addition of which completes Rawls's preliminary account of his theory of social or economic justice, and provides the cap stone of his regime of democratic equality. With it, Rawls hopes that he has provided a theory of justice 'which treats everyone equally as a moral person, and which does not weight men's share in the benefits and burdens of social cooperation according to their social fortune or their luck in the natural lottery' (75).

The difference principle requires of society that, on top of the measures needed to enforce both equal liberty and fair equality of opportunity, the basic institutions of society must be designed so that individuals will be allowed superior economic expectations if and only if those expectations also entail an improvement in the expectations of the worst off. In this way, it will be possible to say that the inequalities permitted are to the advantage of all, or, at least, to the worst off position. The inequalities can be seen as incentives to increase the economic activity of those who in increasing their economic activity increase the efficiency, innovativeness and output of the economy as whole.

The argument for the difference principle comes in three stages. First there is the case for why individuals have no inherent entitlement to their differential rewards, second, there are the reasons for why differentials may be retained when the worst off are benefited and, thirdly, there are the arguments for why differentials that do not benefit the worst off can be appropriated in taxes and redistributed as transfer payments. Also, Rawls openly admits that he offers no proof that the difference principle will have the economic consequence credited to it. He does not claim that there is a significant class of inequalities in economic outcomes whose consequences do as rule boost the position of the worst off (78). However, the difference principle will not be examined on these points here, for the outstanding question remains the viability of Rawls's conception of the economy. If his notion of the economy is invalid then these latter questions will not require investigation. Rather, the issue is to investigate the nature of the link between the difference principle and assumptions regarding the economy.

4

However, before coming to a conclusion, it is necessary to comment on two further stylizations of economic matters. The first concerns that aspect of Rawls's primary goods relevant to this examination of the role of the economy, in other words, income and wealth. Because they are primary goods, it is assumed that each individual, by definition, will want income and wealth to the same degree as every other individual in the market (62). The question is whether this abstraction of economic life represents a significant distortion of both the conventions of actual markets and the correct view of

142

the ethical challenge facing any project to conceive the just economy.

Since every individual wants the primary goods of income and wealth to the same degree, any differences in income and wealth in the outcomes of the economy are not ones individuals will have chosen. (The distinction between the income and wealth which are primary goods and those which are not, and whether such a distinction is possible, will not be taken up here.) With the introduction of primary goods, Rawls has precluded the possibility that differences in economic outcomes might be due simply to preferences. But, why cannot there be differentials of income and wealth simply because some people have chosen to follow a path of, let us say, high commercial reward, whereas others have followed a path of, perhaps, public service or artistic endeavour? In these cases, on the one hand, the differences are not due to social or natural contingencies, greater or lesser exertions, or luck. On the other, the differences considered here are categorical for they cannot necessarily be made commensurable through a model of a leisure-work trade off.

In a manner analogous to the assumption about perfect competition, this stylization of economic life seems to be a serious distortion of both the conventional realities of economic life and the freedom of the individual often assumed to be inherent in market economies. An essential feature of market economies is the diversity of ends pursued. Indeed, it is this possibility of endless diversity, the possibility to pursue ends which are solely personal and particular, and so by definition differentiated from others, which often constitutes a major justification of markets. To reduce all this multiplicity to a single standard of a monetarily defined index in which all have the same interest, is to deny an essential feature of market economies. To suggest that primary goods are only the means and not the ends of economic activity does not get around the problem. For the means to economic ends cannot be reduced to income and wealth, and even when considering income and wealth as a means, there remains the fact that different people will require different quantities of the means of income and wealth.

Rawls does not want to address this diversity of ends in the development of his theory of democratic equality, and avoids doing so with the device of primary goods. In making this abstraction, he advances the construction of his theory in two significant areas. One, the conflation of economic ends to this shared goal of income and wealth, provides both an index for measuring justice, money, and a new criterion, though not the ultimate criterion, of justice, equality. Two, when combined with the assumption of competitive markets, Rawls has gone a long way to reducing

143

economically significant variables to initial assets, as required by his model of justice. For if variation in preferences were allowed then differences in outcomes could not be put down solely to differences in initial assets.

This move to the narrow focus on initial assets entails not just a reduction on one vector of economic life. For not only is it to be just initial assets that determine differences in outcomes, the differences in these assets that account for differences in economic outcomes are all to be morally arbitrary. The exclusion of preferences not only is a further move to limit all relevant factors to the initial assets (assuming that preferences are not already part of an individual's initial assets), it is also the exclusion of a factor which would presumably not be morally arbitrary. (Perhaps, Rawls's thinking could be explained by saying that for him the distribution of initial assets is arbitrary because they are not the result of a Pareto optimal choice procedure, and that procedure is Rawls's only device for establishing the positive validity of a particular outcome. His principles of equality only establish what is not valid.) It might be argued that the requirement within perfect competition theory that both firms and individuals are guided by maximizing motivation might be sufficient to deal with the problem of diverse motivations. Whether this is the case or not, Rawls deems it appropriate to introduce primary goods to ensure against the possibility of diversity, which the difference principle could not handle.

However, the assumption of the perfectly competitive economy and primary goods is not enough to insure that only differentials in initial assets determine differentials in outcome and that all these initial assets are morally arbitrary. A further stylization of economic factors is required. This second abstraction is over the issue of willing or effort. In the inquiry into the matter of preference, it could be said variations in effort were held constant. But what is the theory to make of those who make a greater effort versus those who do not, everything else being equal?

In his discussion of liberal equality, there is the suggestion that differences in economic outcomes that have been in some sense willed, that is to say, are the results of differentials in effort, are not morally arbitrary (73). Yet this special case of the will's contribution is no longer acknowledged in the discussion of democratic equality. For there, the individual has no entitlements to any superior outcomes that may befall him or her, which have their source within himself or herself. The only basis for keeping unequal benefits is if they contribute to the position of the worst off. Perhaps Rawls has concluded upon reaching the specification of democratic equality that differences that are the result of willing, are of a willing that is

144

not free but subject to natural determinations, and so a willing whose effects are morally arbitrary.

Rawls both radically reduces the number of factors that determine differentials of economic outcome and determines that these remaining economically relevant factors are all morally arbitrary. The argument of the paper is that Rawls in reducing the relevant amount of economic influences undermines the credibility of his theory. First, he overlooks a range of economic factors that have a bearing on economic outcomes. Second, there is the suggestion in the discussion of preferences and willing that he also overlooks a category of influences that are economically relevant but are not morally arbitrary.

5

In offering a stylization of the economy wherein perfect competition rules, and where it is possible to abstract out a category of ends, the primary goods, which are the same for everybody, Rawls conceives an economy prior to public regulation which is already very close to the procedures of the just economy. In the regime of democratic equality, public programmes will ensure both that the two principles associated with the openness of positions will be enforced and that the implementation of the difference principle will allow for some inequalities and not others. At the same time, the economy will be operating somehow under its own control so as to conform to the logic of perfect competition. Furthermore, in this economy individuals will share a uniformity of ends due to the assumption concerning primary goods. If one tried to measure what made the greater contribution to the ultimate shape of the society of democratic equality, Rawls's principles of justice or the given character of the economy, it would be hard not to plump for the latter.

Yet the specification of the economy falls outside Rawls's determination of the principles of justice. The principle of efficiency as a contributing feature of Rawls's theory of justice is irrelevant to the issue of justification. Rawls's assumption of competitive markets concerns not their moral/ethical justification but their reality. Yet though the existence of the market as perfectly competitive market is only assumed, in making this assumption, the economy already realizes in large part the structure of the just society. The conception of social justice requires that the actual subjects of justice already exhibit much of the attributes of justice, as well as share a common identity in their common pursuit of primary goods, before the regime of justice is introduced. In other words, the shape that the economy ought to take, and how this shape is to be realized, need not be a subject of the theory of justice.

The requirement that the subject of justice already exhibit the traits of justice is at the heart of Rawls's theory, in the sense that the very argument for the difference principle only works if it is already assumed that the economy has this particular nature. If it is not the case that the economy is the perfectly competitive one, governed by the pursuit of primary goods, then it will not be the case that the introduction of equal opportunity measures will produce an economy with such limited and arbitrary sources for differences in economic performance. And without this limited and arbitrary range of influences determining economic performance, the difference principle cannot operate. If, however, the assumptions regarding the nature of markets are relaxed in favour of a view of competitive markets as an ongoing process, the possibility arises that economic differentials will be due to morally arbitrary factors beyond those considered by Rawls, and differentials will be due to factors that are not morally arbitrary. Once the commitment to perfectly competitive markets is abandoned then the difference principle must also be dropped.

Now, it is the case that Rawls does offer measures, when he considers the implementation of his theory of justice, that attempt to ensure that the economy is competitive. These measures come in his brief discussion of the four branches of his background institutions, the political and legal institutions that will implement the principles of justice (274-284). It could be argued, then, that his assumption is not invalid because he proposes measures to make good that assumption. Yet the limitations of such a defence can be established even before any of the measures Rawls proposes need be considered. In the first place, the proposals for the four branches of government follow the justification of Rawls's theory of justice. Thus if the argument is sequential, in the sense of a straight line of argumentation, where later arguments cannot circle back to justify earlier positions, the measures for implementation, which follow the justification of the principles, cannot at the same time provide the support for the assumptions that the theory requires. But Rawls does not require that his argumentation be strictly sequential, thus it could be said that this criticism can be set aside.

Even so there is the second point that, as Rawls acknowledges, actual economies can only be imperfectly competitive. The reasons for this are many. To start, it is possible to say that certain features of competitive markets are beyond any government's efforts to realize. To this extent, it can be concluded that an attempt to realize the competitive market, as economic theory understands it, is a necessarily futile task. For example, the timeless quality of general equilibrium theory, where individuals have perfect foresight, are features no public measures can realize. Alongside such absolute constraints, there are the partial constraints which Rawls acknowledges when he discusses public competition policy. He recognises that any drive to ensure competition must recognise and respect the limitations imposed upon it by, first, other goals, such as that of maximizing output, and, two, material constraints to do with geography and the preferences of households (276).

6

If the assumption of perfectly competitive markets is abandoned then so too must the principle of efficiency be dropped as a building block in Rawls's theory of justice. The underlying economy to which public measures are to be applied can no longer be taken as manifesting efficiency. The principle of efficiency no longer has a hold in the theory. Are there, then, any aspects to Rawls's theory with an abiding validity upon which an alternative theory could build? The components of his theory of justice that have been rejected, following the critique of the assumption of perfect competition are, to repeat, the difference principle and the principle of efficiency. The argument over the perfectly competitive markets, though, has not undermined the commitment to the notion of equality of opportunity.[8] The difficulty, though, in trying to build upon this principle, is that the answer to the question, 'equality of what?', has been left undetermined with the abandonment of the principle of efficiency. For Rawls equal opportunity is to be realized in the market, because the principle of efficiency provides at least a formal justification of the priority of the market. (There are other social relations which would also satisfy the principle of efficiency.) With the principle of efficiency gone, in Rawlsian terms there is no longer any reason to opt for markets first when seeking to realize equal opportunity.

Yet, while it is not a universal belief, it is within the realm of orthodoxy to suggest that markets should retain the priority they have in Rawls, if for reasons that cannot be given at this point (and which the principle of efficiency does not provide.). Thus, the alternative to Rawls suggested here begins with this assumption of the priority of seeking market solutions first. While a shared commitment to the market is asserted in this new proposal, of course, the nature of that market assumed in the alternative theory is significantly different. This is no end-state equilibrium notion of competition but a view of markets as a continual process of competition. As part of this alternative view of markets is the appreciation that there will be

147

more factors affecting economic outcomes than those to which Rawls limits himself. It is at this point that Rawls's limited notion of equality of opportunity can be introduced and, hopefully, developed further. The first step in realizing the principle of equal opportunity within this new context is to determine which of the further factors affecting economic outcomes are morally arbitrary. If there are morally arbitrary factors beyond those Rawls has identified in his theory, then the question becomes whether the principle of equal opportunity can be so developed as to address them.

For example, consider the case of unemployment. The first determination to make is over the question of responsibility. Is the individual responsible for his or her unemployment? Let us say, he or she is not and that it is due to external factors over which he or she has no or very limited economic influence. It follows that there is a good case for saying that for the sake of equal opportunity, there should be a public intervention to remedy the situation. Given the priority granted to the market, it should be the priority of the relevant public authority both to make good the lapsed participation in the economy and do so in ways that rely on market measures. Yet, how far should this public duty extend? Having given up the notion of primary goods, the theory has no a priori notion of the particular ends which will characterize an individual's market pursuits. No longer are individuals conceived with merely income and wealth in their sights, not to speak of the same amounts of income and wealth. The individual will want any number of things out of the economy. Limits to the public mandate need to be established, or otherwise the public authority faces virtually infinite demands.

One limit the government will face in realizing equality of opportunity will simply be the material constraints that hold in any given circumstance. Thus, the standard of living a public policy of equality of economic opportunity can ensure can only go up to the minimum these constraints allow. While the standard of living of any one individual may go beyond this minimum, the requirements of carrying out an equality of opportunity programme will, at the same time, set maximum limits on the standard of living it will be permissible to earn. For example, income that takes an individual above the publicly guaranteed minimum might be taxed. Still, within these limits, the content of what will be pursued is not predetermined by theory. It will be merely a matter of convention, determined by the actual behaviour of markets supplemented by the activity of public authorities. Consequently, the sketch of this alternative to Rawls can be summed up as the principle of the equal opportunity to freely earn a conventional livelihood within a regulated market economy.[9]

While this principle is not presented here with its complete justification, the brief comments above should show that, when the nature of the economy is refigured, the resulting principles of justice change significantly. Yet this different approach shares some of the same beginnings as are found in Rawls, the commitment to markets and to equality of opportunity. The big disjuncture highlighted here is over the conception of the market. Yet while perfectly competitive equilibrium theory remains at the heart of economic orthodoxy today, it is not an assumption, hopefully, that has extensive dogmatic support within contemporary ethics or political theory.

Notes

1   John Rawls, *A Theory of Justice* (Oxford: Oxford University Press, 1972) . Page references will be given in parentheses in the text.

2   The idea of dividing understandings of market competition between end-state and process views comes from Mark Blaug, *Economic Theory in Retrospect,* fifth edition (Cambridge: Cambridge University Press, 1996), 593. This distinction is set out more fully later in the chapter.

3   Brian Barry, *Theories of Justice, A Treatise on Social Justice*, Volume 1 (Hemel Hempstead: Harvester-Wheatsheaf, 1989), 213. The other line of argument that Rawls uses to justify the difference principle is what Barry refers to as the approach based on the notion of justice as mutual advantage. This is the argument of chapter 3 which relies on the device of the original position. About this latter approach Barry says, 'No other aspect of Rawls's theory has attracted more commentary than his effort to show that the difference principle can be derived from the original position as he specifies it, and it is, I think, safe to say that no other aspect of the theory has met with such uniform rejection' (Ibid., 214).

4   Presumably, as the economy is not contained within his principles of justice its specification must lie outside of his theory of justice. This notion and the consequences of it, if true, will not be addressed directly here.

5   Mark Blaug, *Economic Theory in Retrospect*, 579. See also Geoffrey Brennan, 'The Contribution of Economics', in Robert Goodin and Philip Petit, eds., *A Companion to Contemporary Political Philosophy* (Oxford: Basil Blackwell, 1993), 126-27.
        Blaug also says that perfect competition is compatible with the public ownership of the means of production. Thus Rawls's acceptance of

the compatibility of public ownership with his theory of justice does not in itself necessarily constitute a denial that the economy is perfectly competitive. In other words, the economy need not be completely free to be perfectly competitive. On the matter of the compatibility of social ownership and Walrasian perfectly competitive notions of the economy, Blaug states that in the 1930s Oskar Lange 'taught an entire generation to appreciate the practical import of Walrasian theory employed to support a sort of "bourgeois theory of socialism". According to Lange, socialism was economically feasible if plant managers followed marginal-cost pricing rules and if the central planning board in a socialist regime acted like a Walrasian auctioneer by continually altering prices so as to reduce excess demands to zero' (Blaug, *Economic Theory in Retrospect*, 557).

6   Joan Robinson, *Collected Economic Papers*, Volume 5 (Oxford: Basil Blackwell, 1979), 49-50. Robinson quotes F. H. Hahn, *The Share of Wages in the National Income* (London: Weidenfeld and Nicolson, 1972), no page reference given.

7   Blaug, *Economic Theory in Retrospect*, 593-94. Blaug concludes with a plea that general equilibrium theory be abandoned as part of the discipline of economics. 'I contend that perfect competition is a grossly misleading concept whose only value is to generate an endless series of examination questions. Economics would be a better subject if we discarded it once and for all. Having expunged perfect competition, we ought to follow it by also discarding Walrasian existence proofs and the Invisible Hand Theorem of welfare economics. First of all, everyone admits that these beautiful theorems are mental exercises without the slightest possibility of ever being practically relevant: first-best optima are never actually observed and in a second-best world, it is not in general desirable to fulfil any of the first-best optimum conditions; in other words piecemeal welfare policies may be based on good or bad qualitative judgements but they are not based on rigorous analytical theorems. But once first-best, end-state competition is discarded as irrelevant, as precisely and rigorously wrong, and replaced by process-competition as imprecisely and loosely right, what are we left with? We are left with the content of every chapter in every text book on imperfect or monopolistic competition, on oligopoly, duopoly and monopoly, in short, on industrial organisation as a sub-discipline in economics. In those chapters, firms jostle for advantage by price and nonprice competition, undercutting and out-bidding rivals in the market place by advertising outlays and promotional expenses, launching new differentiated products, new technical processes, new methods of marketing and new organisational forms, and even new reward structures for their employees, all for the sake of head-start profits that they know will soon be eroded' (Ibid., 594).

8   It is worth remembering that Rawls asserts the lexical priority of the principle of equal opportunity, though he does not have in mind the idea that is now being suggested.

9   Richard Dien Winfield proposes a similar idea in *The Just Economy* (New York: Routledge, 1988), 189. Peter Kellner suggests something along these lines in 'More Equality', *The New Statesman*, 17 October 1997. Instead of opportunity, though, he speaks of the equality of access.

9 Passive Patient or Responsible Consumer: Market Values and the Normative Ideal

C.R.E.H. DESCOMBES

Roles are changing within the NHS. Doctors are becoming managers, nurses junior doctors, and the patient with her chart has become the Citizen with her Charter. All these changes are the result, directly or indirectly, of the introduction of market values into the NHS. Whether or not this is to the benefit of all concerned is a matter of continuing debate. In this paper, however, I will argue that the NHS as a whole, and patients in particular, will be better served if patients are encouraged, and even educated, to take on another market-based role, namely, that of consumer. But, it might be protested, that is precisely the role that the NHS reforms were supposed to achieve. Didn't Griffiths, for example, place 'the consumer' centre stage? Possibly so, but as many observers have noted, that particular move, with its shallow emphasis on consumer choice, was little more than a superficial gesture, image building, or, in the uncompromising words of one consultant, 'bullshit'.[1] In this chapter I will argue for something rather more radical, although certainly not new.

In presenting this argument I intend to explore the three main roles available for the individual in the doctor-individual interaction, namely, individual as:

1) Patient;
2) Citizen;
3) Customer/consumer

Underlying this analysis is the conviction that applied philosophy is inherently practical, pragmatic. The focuses is on what can be done in the real world although without losing sight of what we would like done in an ideal world.[2]

152

Doctor and Patient: A Look Beyond the Myth

Medicine, like virtually all other belief systems, has its myths. These stories play an essential role in validating and maintaining not only the overall social order but, as in the case of medicine, the place of particular groups within that wider social structure. However, alongside this positive role myths can, 'if *unexamined and uncriticized*, act ideologically to impede reflection and inhibit emancipation and fundamental change.'[3] The doctor-patient relationship has, in Porter's phrase, 'the ring of myth' about it.[4] This paper begins with a critical examination of the place of this myth in modern medical practice.

The mythical power of the doctor-patient relationship grew out of the need for patients to have faith in the person of the doctor as healer. Before the advent of biologic medicine with its powerful arsenal of drugs and surgical procedures, there was very little that the doctor could offer but his caring, and often commanding, bedside manner. In that situation the practice of medicine was virtually all about a desirable clinical relationship.[5] Nowadays, the situation is very different. Not only does modern medicine work on patients 'who don't know their doctors or don't like their doctors' but it requires such an army of health care providers that, as Bok has observed, the trust underpinning the notion of a one-to-one and ongoing doctor patient relationship is no longer possible.[6] Nevertheless, until quite recently the 'normative ideal' for the relationship was of the paternalistic expert on whom patients could and should implicitly rely. How suited is that normative ideal to modern health care, including that provided within the NHS?

The image of the patient is one of passivity and compliance. Patients are expected to 'follow doctors' orders', those who question are termed 'difficult', and medical and nursing personnel strongly disapprove of 'non-compliance'. Yet medicine is increasingly complex and many procedures are potentially risky, even life-threatening. Furthermore, the principle of autonomy, a central tenet of medical ethics, along with the need for patients to give their informed consent, calls for health care users to be both questioning and actively involved in all aspects of treatment. Then too, doctors' decisions are influenced not only by the needs of the individual patient but by a range of interests and concerns - professional, academic, business, or personal - beyond those of treating any one patient. All this suggests that individuals needs to take some responsibility for looking after their own health care interests. Indeed, this has been the experience of some groups of NHS users who found that their particular needs and interests were persistently poorly understood and consequently ill-met. Thus, for example, the long-term disabled, ethnic minorities, and women, have all found it necessary to move beyond the passive, compliant patient model to the position where they have taken responsibility for representing their care needs, thereby safeguarding their own health and well being; less patients and more consumers. It is also worth noting that elderly persons requiring long term nursing care increasingly find the NHS unwilling to meet their needs and in this situation they are forced into the role of consumers having to buy their nursing care from the private sector.[7] (There appears to be little widespread and sustained objection to this latter state of affairs.) All these developments lead to the question: should the consumer/customer model become the new normative ideal for the individual-doctor interaction?

Against the NHS Consumer, for the NHS Citizen

Definitely not, is the almost instinctive response to this question, especially from many moral philosophers who see themselves as defenders and supporters of the NHS. Among their objections to this model they point out that: consumers are selfish and demanding, neither of which traits have any place within the NHS; although often ignorant about their real health care needs, consumers would think themselves 'always right' and so insist unreasonably on their doctor simply complying with their every ill-considered whim and wish; by placing the interests of the consumer above all else the model takes no account of the doctor's rights as an independent agent with her or his own professional and moral commitments.[8] This last objection is from a distinguished bioethicist well used to the concept of the consumer in that most consumer-oriented society, the USA. Returning, however, to this side of the Atlantic one suggested moral alternative to the patient, if indeed such is needed, is not the NHS consumer but the NHS citizen.

In analysing these two roles the idea of citizen is often presented as morally superior to that of consumer. Whereas, as already noted, it is widely perceived that consumers have no thought other than the satisfaction of their own wants, the citizen, on the other hand, recognises the wider implications of their choices, the meaning and moral value of those individual decisions. It is almost as if we are consumers in our fallen state, whereas our perfect condition is as citizens. It is the citizen, not the consumer, who should inherit the NHS. But what does such an idea mean in practice?

Although the concept of the citizen as an individual who belongs to a particular state, that is owes allegiance to and receives protection from their country, is reasonably well understood, in its more ideological form, involving commitment and bonding, an active engagement in a political community, the concept is almost foreign, perhaps in the common view rather more American or French than British. Indeed it has been noted that 'in this society, citizenship is an archaic term. It is not part of the language of everyday life. Its value for understanding this life is not evident either.'[9]

In reality 'citizen' has become synonymous not with responsibility to, and even self-sacrifice for, the good of the wider community, but with personal rights. This is certainly the focus of the so-called Citizens' Charter where the emphasis is all on what patients have the right to expect when they visit their GP surgery or hospital. How much does the narrowly rights-focused citizen patient understand of responsibilities to, solidarity with, other citizen patients, or citizen doctors, or citizen taxpayers? The increasing level of demand, and particularly for trivial needs, suggests there is very little understanding of this principle. At the time of writing this paper two new drugs are about to come onto the market.[10] Both are designed to meet problems that for many are little more than annoying although for a few they can be deeply distressing and, in the case of obesity, life threatening. However, it is anticipated that there will be such a huge demand from citizen patients for one of these drugs that the resources of the NHS will be stretched to breaking point. There is little confidence that a spirit of citizenship will restrain the majority of potential users and consequently the government has called for a moratorium on NHS prescribing.

With such an apparently impoverished understanding of who and what the citizen really is the concept can have very little practical moral impact. If the term refers to some idealised, and perhaps never fully realised, past then it is of doubtful value in helping the individual interact responsibly and effectively with health care professionals.

Perhaps the apologists for citizenship will object to this argument. They may claim, and doubtless quite rightly, that an honourable concept has been hijacked by the Right and diluted into something closer to a mere egoistic consumer. Regrettable as this watered down version may be it is probably closer to the reality of citizenship in Britain today. Pragmatism requires we recognize this unpalatable reality not merely to bewail a lost ideal but in order that we might explore practical moral alternatives. There is reason to suggest that the negative, demonised image of the consumer is itself a somewhat one-sided view. Just as there is nowadays less moral content to

155

the concept 'citizen' there is potentially more to the concept 'consumer'.

Another View of the Consumer

Although notions of citizen and citizenship may have atrophied, the notion of consumer is undoubtedly alive and kicking. 'We have no serious difficulty thinking of ourselves as consumers.'[11] Nevertheless, the value of this concept as the normative ideal for individual-doctor interactions requires some clarification simply because 'consumer' has such a wide range of conflicting meanings.

We have already noted the very negative image that the concept carries: the consumer as greedy, selfish, unconstrained by moral considerations. In other words the consumer represents the values of the market economy, which values are undermining the public service and collectivist values on which the NHS is founded. This argument, however, takes no account of the fact that market values have operated within the NHS from the beginning.

The NHS is at many levels a business like any other business although more a complex variety of different markets operating under the one NHS umbrella than a single enterprise. It is also far bigger than most, employing hundreds of thousands of staff, and buying and selling many millions of pounds of goods and services. Whilst not operating as a profit making organisation the Service, whether in its role as consumer or supplier, has always had a moral responsibility to conduct the majority of these transactions on market based principles of efficiency and value for money.

Other market-based consumer values have long operated within its walls. Thus doctors, more especially consultants, were only persuaded to give their support to the NHS by promises of large amounts of money.[12] From the earliest days patients, without the constraints of having to pay for their health care, were, as the first Minister of Health Aneurin Bevan observed, soon pouring cascades of medicine down their throats, apparently well beyond any medical need. And, in the light of this regrettable reality, much to his dismay Bevan had to impose a shilling prescription charge in order to reduce the cascade to more manageable levels.[13] In both cases it appears that doctors and patients demonstrated those selfish characteristics that are now offered as reasons against encouraging the patient as consumer in the reformed NHS. However, such selfishness is by no means the only value guiding the modern consumer.

In a powerful critique of both egalitarianism and natural-rights libertarianism, one eminent philosopher argues that this stereotypical image of the egoistic consumer is a caricature. Rather than being motivated purely by selfishness consumers can be, and often are, guided by altruism and sympathy. He goes further and claims that market systems actually instill sensitivity to the needs and preferences of others. This is because market systems operating within Western societies are based on the autonomous person - not selfish, more self-possessed, with a distinct self-identity, authentic, self-directed and, to some significant degree, self-created. 'The autonomy fostered by market orders is, then, that of independence and responsibility, not that of the free-floating sovereign self, or the rootless author of the *acte gratuite*.'[14] Whether or not we are prepared to go as far as Gray in arguing the moral case for the autonomous consumer there is no doubt that the consumer can and often does behave in a responsible and highly moral fashion.

The consumer activist has a long and honourable history. From their earliest appearance in mid-eighteenth century America where they were active in opposing colonial exploitation right up to the present day ethical consumer movement, their activities have always been morally driven. The actions of these consumers demonstrate that 'right and wrong, damaging and beneficial, useless and useful, needs and wants are concepts that cannot be written out of consumption.'[15] How practised is the passive patient in applying these ideas to their use of the NHS?

Passive Patient or Responsible Consumer

Patients may be passive in the sense of resigned and even submissive but they can equally well be demanding and selfish. Along with stories of the grateful patient who happily accepts whatever the doctor can do, GPs are always able to recount numerous tales of malingerers and time-wasters who fill their waiting rooms or call them out in the small hours of the morning, apparently quite unaware of the needs of other patients or even of the doctors themselves; hospital doctors can equally well tell of accident and emergency departments cluttered with patients aggressively demanding attention for some minor condition. Inasmuch as personal responsibility and involvement are not part of the role of the passive patient such passivity may perversely tend to encourage selfishness and aggression.

Thus the passive patient may take considerable exception to being told, for example, that their condition is self-limiting and will not be helped by antibiotics. However, as doctors are under pressure to reduce their prescribing of ineffective or unnecessary treatments they find themselves in the position of having to encourage and educate those very patients to understand this new state of affairs.[16] In other words, it would appear that the NHS needs people to accept some responsibility for their own health care: not so much passive patient as responsible consumer.

Furthermore, the objection that those requiring the services of the NHS are not typical consumers insofar as such a typical consumer 'is assumed to be adult, healthy, able to reason, informed or in the position to be informed',[17] carries little weight. Consumers come in all shapes and sizes, all ages, states of health, and reasoning ability. The fact that those requiring health care from the NHS may not be in the peak of physical, mental, or emotional condition is no basis for arguing that they cannot be responsible consumers.

Of course it goes without saying that there may be health situations in which an individual is absolutely unable to take any responsibility even though, in other circumstances, they certainly would wish to do so. The genuine accident or emergency calls for health care professionals to act speedily and in a somewhat authoritarian manner. We all accept this licence in the immediate urgency of the situation. However, such an approach should be the exception, not the rule, for the majority of doctor-individual encounters. Most of these are instigated by the 'patient' and, even when requiring further treatment, fall into the category of so-called cold or elective procedures. In these situations NHS users must be recognized as autonomous, responsible individuals, moral agents who are able not only to take a full part in decisions regarding their own health but also to appreciate the wider implications of their health care 'purchasing' decisions, indeed for certain of those implications better able than any outsider no matter how expert in their own field.[18] It is this sense of personal responsibility and involvement that should be encouraged in NHS users.

When health care professionals, especially doctors, acknowledge the Service user as responsible consumer then even the vexed issue of choice appears in a very different light and with the potential for a rather more positive outcome. It is no longer the superficial window-dressing of the NHS reforms but now offers users the opportunity to consider real alternatives. The NHS may be a monopoly provider for the vast majority of those requiring health care but within that monopoly a considerable range of choice is available. Thus, for example, on the question of choosing the best consultant to perform a particular operation the standard procedure is for the GP alone to make the referral choice. It is not considered appropriate to invite the patient to participate in that decision, instead they must simply trust that the doctor will make the decision 'in the patient's best interests'. However, for the responsible consumer that situation will be very different. Although fully aware that the professional's expert knowledge must be respected, the responsible consumer will, nonetheless, expect to be involved in making this and all other such important treatment choices. Shared decision-making is no longer a favour or gift the doctor may or may not decide to confer but recognized by all as the right and duty of the responsible consumer in consultation with their medical practitioner.

Conclusion

The NHS is under enormous pressure as it struggles to meet the increasingly costly demands on its resources. Passive but expectant patients and rights-focused citizens do not take kindly to the notion that the Service cannot meet their every health care need. However, it doesn't even take a responsible consumer, merely a reasonably intelligent one, to recognize that the range and quality of goods available in Woolworth's will never match that available from Harrods. The NHS can never be the Harrods of health care yet it can still do an excellent and much needed job. But this may only be possible if those who use it are recognized and encouraged in their role as consumers - not the caricature selfish and overly demanding consumer, but responsible consumers who understand what service the NHS is able to provide and are prepared to work with it in order to ensure that it can continue to provide that service. In other words, the sort of consumers who every day, as they bank ethically, invest ethically, shop ethically, do so in the knowledge that the consumption decisions they make affect not only their lives, but the lives of their family, and the wider community.

It may not meet the ideal of the mythical citizen; nonetheless the role of responsible consumer is rather more than a pragmatic compromise. It is a well-thought out moral position that not only positively benefits the health of the individual consumer but works for the good of the NHS and the community as a whole - something rather closer to the ideal envisaged by the founding lights than has perhaps been the case up to now.

Notes

1   S. Harrison, D. J. Hunter, G. Marnoch, and C. Pollitt, *Just Managing: Power and Culture in the National Health Service* (London, Macmillan, 1992), pp. 56-57; C. Paton, *Competition and Planning in the NHS: The Danger of Unplanned Markets* (London, Chapman & Hall, 1992), pp. 14-19.

2   B. Almond & D. Hill, (eds) *Applied Philosophy: Morals and Metaphysics in Contemporary Debate* (London, Routledge, 1991) pp. 1-2.

3   S. Pattison, *The Faith of the Managers: When Management Becomes Religion,* (London, Cassell, 1997) p.53., emphasis added; A. Wiener *Magnificent Myth,* (Oxford, Pergamon Press, 1978) p.162; M. Midgley *The Ethical Primate: Humans, Freedom and Morality* (London, Routledge, 1994) p.117.

4   R. Porter, *The Greatest Benefit to Mankind: a Medical History of Humanity from Antiquity to the Present* (London, Harper Collins, 1997) p.669.

5   R. Porter, pp.9-10; also D. and R. Porter, *Patient's Progress: Doctors and Doctoring in Eighteenth Century England* (Oxford, Blackwell, 1989).

6   J.D. Lantos, *Do We Still Need Doctors?* (London, Routledge, 1997) p.4; S. Bok *Lying* (New York, Vintage Books, 1989) p.233.

7   Chris Combes (author C.R.E.H. Descombes) 'Make the Young Pay for the Old' in *Health Service Journal,* 30 April 1998, p.29.

8   T. Sorrell 'Morality, Consumerism and the Internal Market in Health Care' in *Journal of Medical Ethics* 23 (1997), pp.71-76; D. W. Brock *Life and Death: Philosophical Essays in Biomedical Ethics* (Cambridge University Press, 1993) p.58.

9   Wexler quoted in Y. Gabriel and T. Lang *The Unmanageable Consumer: Contemporary Consumption and its Fragmentation* (London, Sage, 1995) p.174.

10   One for erectile dysfunction or impotence, the other for obesity.

11   See Y. Gabriel and T. Lang, op. cit.

12   C. Webster *The National Health Service: a Political History* (Oxford, Oxford University Press, pp.26-28.

13   R. Klein *The New Politics of the NHS, 3rd Edition* (London, Longman, 1995), p.31.

14   J. Gray *The Moral Foundations of Market Institutions* (London, The IEA Health and Welfare Unit, 1992) p.25.

15   Gabriel and Lang, see footnote 9, p.171.

16   See for example the Patient Information Poster and the introductory material offered in *Doctor* 3 September 1998, p.1.

17   T. Sorrell, op. cit.

18   For a thoughtful discussion on the ethical questions raised by understanding the needs of the individual in the context of the family see H.L. Nelson and J.L.Nelson *The Patient in the Family* (London, Routledge, 1995).

10 Relocating the 'Ethical Consumer'

TERRY NEWHOLM

Introduction

In the last quarter of the twentieth century interest in consumer theory has grown significantly within and across disciplines. The recent notion of a more active and discerning consumer has elicited widely differing responses. So whilst the political theorist David Pepper[1] dismissively associates 'eco-consumerism' with the social and environmental degradation of Thatcher's market liberalism, Bido Schlegelmilch[2] celebrates the active consumer as the marketing discipline's solution to all ills and Rob Harrison[3] advocates consumer power as key element in a strategy for change.

It is against this contentious background that terms seeking to describe consumer activism have progressed through 'green consumerism', 'socially conscious consumerism' to 'eco-consumerism'. Recently the term 'ethical consumerism' has been adopted by some activist organisations, market researchers and academics to encompass a range of consumer behaviours where people seem to act upon more than self-interest.

My aim here is to address the assertion that ethical consumerism can be incorporated into a market liberal perspective and briefly consider the comprehensive political critique of consumer activism set out by Pepper. Drawing on these considerations and my own research I will discuss the context and propositions of the phenomenon to contribute towards a political philosophy of ethical consumerism. I shall assume the ideologies discussed here to be coherent within their own terms and am concerned only with the relationship between ideology and ethical consumerism.

Classical Economics: The Individual Consumer in the Market Economy

'Consumer sovereignty' is one of the implicit presumptions of market

162

liberalism. As the theory was provocatively set out in the 1940s by Ludwig von Mises it would initially form an attractive basis for the analysis of ethical consumerism. R.A.Gonse[4] summarises the economist's position thus:

> The heart of his argument is that if strict *laissez-faire* capitalism exists, wherein the state enforces juristic laws and leave the operation of natural laws unhampered, then consumer sovereignty will rule over all, with the rational interests of all other classes being harmonized with it in the long run. In more detail, the consumers' rational wants, as expressed by effective consumer demand in product markets, ultimately (the exact meaning of 'ultimately' being left unclear) will determine all prices; self-interested entrepreneurs, factor owners, savers and investors will voluntarily and rationally calculate and choose courses of action in the light of price facts; and so effective consumer demand will govern 'all economic phenomena' and optimally satisfy itself.

Additionally the rhetoric which underpins ethical consumerism is often similar to that of market liberalism. Enoch Powell,[5] for instance, paragon of market liberal theorists, extols the market as a super-democracy.

> Everyone who goes into a shop and chooses one article instead of another is casting a vote in the economic ballot box: with thousands or millions of others that choice is signalled through to production and investment and helps to mould the world just a tiny fraction nearer to people's desire. In this great and continuous general election of the free economy nobody, not even the poorest, is disenfranchised: we are all voting all the time.

Using a similar electoral metaphor Paul Ekins,[6] an advocate of ethical consumerism, points to the advantages of the market in situations where *individual preferences* are to be recorded.

> The market is a most useful institution for individual, decentralised decision-making. With no intermediary bureaucracy it enables people as consumers to express their preferences directly, knowing not only that their purchasing power will secure the product or service of their choice, but also that it will act as an economic vote to encourage producers to deliver more of the same.

It is, therefore, both tempting and not unreasonable to associate ethical consumerism with market liberalism. However, I shall argue that prominent adherents of the grand theory construct scenarios which disregard the notion of 'ethics' in consumption and that, more so than in general consumer

163

situations, it is difficult to conceive an individualised ethical consumer. I will also suggest that many of the concepts that inform ethical consumers can be shown to be contrary to those of market liberalism and therefore that it is questionable whether the ideology needs or can sustain the inclusion of ethical consumerism.

Market Liberalism and the Ethical Consumer

I want to begin with a brief sketch of the ideal market liberal ethical consumer and then move to a critique of the notion. Clearly the central claim of the ideology must remain, that self-interest generates wealth and has beneficial but unintended outcomes. In this utilitarian concept it is the value of the generation and 'trickle down' of wealth that underpins the argument in favour of liberalising the market. In so far as this wealth creation commands general support, and it is now widely accepted that it does, it is deemed to be superior to any other system. Whatever outcome arises from market distribution is justified, by market liberals, in terms of the need to maintain self-interested competition which leads to general material progress and the greater good.

Market research organisations have constructed a concept of the ethical consumer and this would seem the most appropriate formulation for present purposes. According to Mintel[7] ethical consumers are concerned with a number of environmental issues, animal welfare, fair trade, and to a lesser but growing extent, the adverse effects of armament manufacture and general corporate social policy. At this point it will be assumed that producers are self-interested and willing to respond to consumer preferences whether or not they conform to this concept of an ethical consumer. An accommodation of ethical consumers could therefore be made in terms of individual consumers 'voting' in the free market and self-interested producers responding.

The final point to make before progressing is that in this ideology ethical consumers would seek information to make rational decisions but would not attempt to regulate the market through collective action or legislation. Any such regulation would be seen to cause inefficiencies in the market and damage wealth production. Furthermore, such collective action to overrule the market would be well-meaning but misguided moral sanctimony based on an over-estimation of individual human ability to rationalise issues. Pressure groups are an anathema in market liberalism.

I will now consider the relationship between ethical consumers and the key market liberal tenets of self-interest and individualism. Following this I will make a comparison between the general underlying values of market

164

liberalism and ethical consumerism.

Self-interest

I might usefully begin with Adam Smith's classic formulation in the *Wealth of Nations* published in 1776 of the 'invisible hand' of the market.

> It is not from the benevolence of the butcher, the brewer, or the baker, that we expect our dinner, but from their regard to their own interest.

In considering altruism and self-interest here in relation to Smith's work I assume D. D. Raphael's understanding of 'the Adam Smith problem'.[8] Thus Smith speaks of benevolence but it is self-interest that produces wealth. When Smith makes great play in *Moral Sentiments* of the human capacity for sympathy it is strictly in relation to the understanding of the actions of others. Aside from this, Raphael argues, the notion of sympathy in Smith's work has a limited role; sympathy is not a motivation but a source of moral feeling necessary to social cohesion. In addition, the market creates bonds through interdependence. In this way rational self-interest is for Smith a moral good. It is to be approved but is not of the highest order or worthy of 'warm admiration'.[9]

This understanding coincides with recent free-market approaches to environmental issues. Terry Anderson and Donald Leal[10] write:

> Free market environmentalism views man [sic] as self interested. This self interest may be enlightened to the extent that people are capable of setting aside their own well being for close relatives and friends or that they may be conditioned by moral principles. But beyond this, good intentions will not suffice to produce good results. Developing an environmental ethic may be desirable, but it is unlikely to change basic human nature. Instead of intentions, good resource stewardship depends on how well social institutions harness self-interest through individual incentives.

It is not, therefore, that we are to understand all action as self-interested but that it is self-interest that is the decisive motivation. The above quotation is from a general statement of free market *environmentalism*. It seems to me, however, appropriate to a wider understanding of market liberalism in relation to the present subject. This is both because environmental concerns are a substantial component of ethical consumerism but also because there are theoretical similarities with other issues. Such a conceptualisation is distinctly behaviourist and finds further echoes in the more recent work of Gordon Foxall.[11] The consumer, he argues, will buy green, or presumably 'ethical' products, when the benefits obtainable from buying other products are equalled or surpassed.

In the same way when, from an overtly political standpoint, Samuel Brittan sought to establish the 'green power of market forces' he did not rely on any supposed good will among consumers.[12] He espoused 'primarily and mostly' the notion, championed by Pearce,[13] of inducements and penalties dependent on the costing of 'externalities' and comprehensive self-interested private property rights. I see the latter as the more purely market liberal approach.

It is not the intention here to evaluate these market liberal formulations but to note that the ethical consumer is *conspicuously absent*. Whatever problems are advanced the solution lies, in so far as consumers are concerned, in a self-interested response to particular market conditions.

Individual Preferences?

Market liberals hold an individualist 'vision' of humanity; Keith Joseph,[14] for instance, prefers not to speak of society but of the 'sum of its individual members'. This is important not only in their understanding of humanity but also in the claim that the market responds to the *majority* of people's preferences in a superior manner to democracy. Hence Friedman's[15] assertion that the market produces unanimity without conformity whilst democracy produces conformity without unanimity. Democracy, whilst a necessary adjunct to the free market, must be strictly limited to deciding choices where conformity is *essential*.

Here I will consider the notion of individualised ethical consumer preferences both theoretically and empirically. Firstly, assuming that ethical consumers take action purposefully, in *theory* three features of their potential decision making environment are apparent:

1.   Scope of application - deploying ethics within contemporary society where consumption is a major feature of an individual's life is a potentially extensive task.
2.   Irresolvability - most issues are complex and where multiple issues arise may be simply irresolvable in any satisfactory sense.
3.   Recurrent decisions - decisions once made are susceptible to

re-examination due to changing circumstances.

In illustration of these points consider when concerns for the environment are coupled with ones for fair trade. In some way these concerns are applicable to *every* product or service yet *conflicts* can arise between a concern to trade fairly with majority world countries, to promote their economies, and environmental problems of excessive transportation. These fine judgements might need *reassessment* if a hitherto boycotted company adopted an acceptable 'ethical' policy or challenges arose to the policy of a supposedly 'ethical' company. In terms of ethical consumers actually sending their intended message to the producer these decisions become even more complicated.[16] Of course few ethical consumers are so dedicated to their task as actually to approach their consumption in the way I have described, but even in less daunting circumstances individualistic decision making about the ethics of purchases would be at best grossly inefficient, with many people replicating decision making processes, and at worst pathological.

Current research in this area is seemingly contradictory. Focus group research has suggested that ethical consumers feel isolated in what they are doing.[17] This may well support a notion of consumers with individualised preferences. However, Deirdre Shaw[18] who is currently analysing a survey of more than 1400 subscribers to *Ethical Consumer* magazine finds that membership of single issue organisations is exceptionally high. Such organisations are cited by these consumers as significant sources of information. In addition Shaw's data suggest that family, friends and colleagues provide important motivations towards ethical consumption.

My own current research which has developed sixteen in-depth case studies suggests a similar picture. Two cases might illustrate this. The first is a churchgoer who is a member of a small fair trade group and avidly reads the church magazine. When I first met her informally she told me about majority world debt in some detail. Subsequently, during a semi-structured interview, I asked how she knew about this issue. She referred me to the magazine article, which closely corresponded to what she had told me, and particularly the conclusion. This as she explained virtually instructed her to move her account to the Cooperative Bank which had not been involved in the debt crisis and had an 'ethical policy'. Here there is one major source of authoritative information and the ideas on what is appropriate action are mostly generated remotely from this consumer.

In contrast to this would be the young man who with his partner was quite explicitly part of a group who informally but regularly discussed how they should live in consumer capitalism. They were members of a number of pressure groups like Friends of the Earth and drew on ideas from these organisations. They acted these out on their allotments and in their consumption patterns. Because they are active in these organisations both locally and nationally they drew on their experiences in the discussions which inform group policy. In this case there are many sources of information, they seemed to me to be more critically appraised, and the ethical consumers took a small but significant part in regenerating the ideas.

In *practice*, therefore, initial research suggests two decision making modes:

1. didactic, where consumers are introduced to a collective understanding of ethical consumption, and
2. dialectic, where ethical consumers are engaged both in a process of purchasing with ethical beliefs and understandings and in the social processes which construct and reconstruct the 'contemporary narratives' of ethical consumerism.

Of course there are those who have begun to deploy the ideas of ethical consumerism beyond the particular products or services where the original concept arose but who cannot, as yet, be said to be linked into any dialectic process. They may perhaps be said to be internalising the ideas. However, the two conditions seem distinct in the sense that consumers in one mode would not comfortably transfer to the other, nor would they necessarily react similarly in a given situation. By this I mean that my research suggests that some people react favourably to clear 'answers' whereas others react cynically against argument that they find too simplistic.[19]

However, both may experience a degree of isolation in the more or less individual purchasing process. The above understanding certainly offers an alternative to the individualised notions of public choice necessary to market liberalism and places the ethical consumer in a more social framework. In this way they may be viewed as complementary to, rather than separate from, democratic activism and other forms of consumer / producer activism.

Pepper[20] uses the term 'mythology' to describe the collective understandings of eco-consumers. Whereas he wishes to signify falsehood, by the use of the word 'narratives' I wish to reflect the complexity of the issues involved and the tentative, partial and sometimes conflicting nature of the resolutions. This draws on the theoretical position of ethical consumers set out above and parallels the already changing strategies of ethical consumerism as exemplified by the shift in emphasis of many activists from alternative production and retailing to political and consumer pressure on high street retailers.

I would therefore prefer to think of ethical consumers being more or less integrated into the production of *collective narratives* which influence, but do not determine, their *isolated* behaviour in the market.

Ethical Consumers and Moral Entrepreneurs?

However, in market liberalism it is clearly not only consumers who are presumed to maximise. David Pepper[21] locating consumer pressure in market liberalism says:

> Consumer pressure for environment-friendly products will play a big part [and] *capital will respond to this market.* (emphasis added)

Taking this line of argument further Milton Friedman[22] writes of producers:

> He [sic] has a right to promote what he regards as desirable moral objectives *only with his own money.* (emphasis added)

Conversely, part of the argued value of ethical consumerism is to encourage a morality in business.[23] Whilst there are of course those business people who have characterised their response to ethical consumers simply as good business, there seems to me to be something more fundamental demanded. Whether the notion of moral entrepreneurs is naive or not is not in question here. A tension arises within market liberalism with the very concept of the public good being served by producers balancing profit maximisation with a moral concern for society. In such an arrangement it is difficult to see what would differentiate the 'invisible hand' thesis from say the One Nation imperative of attention to circumstance.

An alternative approach has been to argue that all behaviour is self-interested. In this, the behaviour of ethical consumers could be construed, say, as having a long-term self-interest. However, I take this as being a primarily a device within the Business Studies discipline which is not strongly paralleled in political philosophy.[24] In addition, as Amitai Etzioni has I think successfully argued, the concept of self-interest is so weakened by the inclusion of all behaviour as to become meaningless.[25] This device, he argues, simply serves to diminish our scope for analysis of what is a complex set of sometimes conflicting motives. Additionally, I suggest that such a modification may be disregarded because it strays seriously from the original and substantive ideology of market liberalism briefly set out in the beginning of this paper.

The General Values of Market Liberalism and Ethical Consumerism: A Comfortable Fit?

Pepper[26] draws parallels between some ideas in consumerist strategy and market liberalism. So for instance he speaks of the individualisation of responsibility for environmental damage implied by eco-consumer theories. This is clearly in line with Friedman's[27] free market analysis. However, it is perhaps easier to indicate tensions between the tenets of market liberalism and the issues espoused by ethical consumers. Here I shall outline some of these issues and offer what I intend as plausible ideological readings which are contrary to market liberalism.

The aims of fair trade seem to me to conflict with the limited notion of freedom advocated by market liberals. Fair trade projects aim, among other things, to increase the income to the primary producer, especially to provide and improve collective social projects. This is to widen the real options open to those in these communities. Such a concept is clearly more in line with Hattersley's[28] view of *positive* freedom than Joseph's[29] tightly defined liberty.

Unease about the production and supply of armaments finds echoes, I would suggest, in Tawney's[30] concept of 'social purpose in production'.

Animal welfare arguments against factory farming which underpin much of the move among consumers towards veganism, vegetarianism and an omnivorous diet based on free range animal products surely run counter to the notion of the self-interested and efficient exploitation of animals embodied in Thatcher's deregulation of farming.

Issues of child labour, especially when related to profits realised on low cost, high exchange value goods, seem to run counter to the notion of unavoidable or advantageous inequality. They can be seen as embodying notions of unacceptable wealth and poverty which would be closer to Galbraith's[31] indignation at 'extreme poverty side by side with great wealth' than Hayek's[32] dignified poverty in a world of unintended inequality.

The view that we cannot continue unregulated material exploitation on which environmentally conscious consumerism draws seems to have more in common with Pepper's[33] espousal of eco-socialism than the philosophy of

170

laissez faire.

In other words each of the issues addressed can be seen as counter to market liberal theory or relates to an outcome where the 'free' market is deemed to have failed. This is not to argue that the market system does not have merit, that the issues are correctly understood by ethical consumers or that ethical consumerism represents an homogeneous ideology but to point out that there is a considerable ideological tension between the construct of market liberalism and that of much of ethical consumerism.

I have argued that, beyond upholding the laws, ethics in *market dealings* is not a motivation on which the market liberal project relies. Additionally I have observed a necessary collective element in ethical consumer narratives, narratives which are themselves frequently contrary to concepts essential to market liberalism. To note that some individuals may bring ethics to their consumer decisions and that self-interested producers will take advantage of this opportunity, but to argue that this is incidental to the production of general good, is to create no real tension within market liberalism. To accommodate a notion of ethical consumers, however, as a necessary part of a market system must imply, I have argued, a failure in practice and a significant dilution of the ideology. Classical economics is ill equipped to accommodate other than maximising consumers.

Additionally if it were accepted that market systems have tendencies towards moral minimalism, as argued by Patrick Shaw in this publication, then a further implication could be drawn. It is inevitable that the efforts of ethical consumers would be subverted by the workings of the market. In this sense market liberalism is inevitably contrary to any notion of a consequentially effective ethical consumerism. Herein is the concept of 'the consumer as activist doomed to struggle endlessly against the odds'.[34]

Pepper's Critique of Ethical Consumerism

A 'Protest of the Wealthy'

Pepper[35] and others dismiss ethical consumerism as a protest of the wealthy and therefore in some way not worthy of consideration. Such a dismissal stereotypes an heterogeneous group. Certainly current research confirms that ethical consumers receive either a higher than an average income or choose to 'downshift' and in that sense they are not poor. However, implicit in the argument that consumer activism is a 'middle-class' phenomenon must be a notion that the proletarian majority would consume differently; by choice, only for need. Such an idea is difficult to sustain. High involvement in the National Lottery, for instance, suggests as, Baudrillard[36] argues, a general eagerness to consume. There is an eagerness in newly developed countries to join consumerism[37] and even socialists are not immune.[38] There is therefore no inherent reason not to investigate a 'protest of the wealthy' and perhaps, every good reason.

More immediately the actions of the wealthy protesters do have effects and these, as I shall acknowledge, are sometimes detrimental to the poor. In the broadest sense an understanding of the processes of ethical consumerism seems to me to be as important to those who espouse the interests of the poor as to any others.

A Constituent of False Consciousness

Pepper's concern with false consciousness is that people will return home from a shopping spree with their jar of fair traded coffee and a pack of recycled paper kitchen rolls believing that both economic exploitation and environmental problems have been resolved. Clearly contradictions and misconceptions of scale are likely to exist and may mitigate against consumers adopting more radical views.[39]

Conversely, however, empirical evidence also seems to point to a radicalising tendency. Here again I refer to a number of my case studies as examples. Having been introduced relatively recently to the arguments justifying fair trade products one respondent asked staff at her holiday destination about their pay. She was shocked. I had little doubt but that this changed her understanding on inequality. An academic who was concerned for animal welfare was introduced to issues of fair trade through the literature. He said that since then he has increasingly 'got into' fair trade. Ethical consumers ask challenging questions when they shop. In these ways understanding of one situation can be transferred to another, cross over into seemingly unrelated concerns and challenge the perceptions of others.

Although my study is limited in its exploration of change over time, it seems probable that some ethical consumers, whilst espousing different concerns from time to time, more or less constantly limit their total attention to these. For instance one of my respondents became less proactive as a 'green' consumer as she increased her attention towards animal rights. Others to differing extents broaden their concerns and very few significantly 'downshift'. Thus, however limited, I think it is unbalanced to ignore radicalising tendencies in ethical consumerism.

An Ineffective Strategy for Change

Some commentators see ethical consumerism as a strategy for change.[40] Arguments about the ineffectiveness of consumer activism revolve around its conservative nature. There is no reason to suggest from my study other than that, where they intend consequences, for the most part ethical consumers seek to modify, not destroy capitalism. However, in political terms, the strategy is no more vulnerable to the charge of ineffectiveness than any other gradualist approach.

In so far as ethical consumerism is seen as an isolated action of isolated individuals, of course, it appears particularly weak.[41] However, as I have argued, most consumer action is based on a collective narrative and/or orchestrated campaign and, however remotely, some legislative possibility is implied. The consideration of the phenomenon in isolation is therefore not appropriate.

Working towards an Eco-Socialist Utopia

Pepper[42] offers a critique of oppositional strategies which are found in consumer capitalism. Each is valued in terms of its ideological distance from and implied criticism of capitalism. Consumerist strategies are rejected as set out above, cooperative and mutual business structures are given a qualified support to the extent that they may prefigure anarcho-socialist forms, and secessionist strategies such as local exchange trading systems (LETS) are endorsed. The constituency for oppositional forces is the working class globally and progressives within these movements.

In practice it is not as easy to differentiate between strategies. Many ethical consumers encountered in my study were involved, for instance, in the defence of the mutual societies of which they are members against recent attacks. They often preferentially patronise cooperatives and among them are members of LETS. Those involved in ethical consumption are predominantly the same radicals as would otherwise be approved of by many on the left as social heroes; a radical solicitor, radical teachers, members of worker cooperatives, a campaigning actor/playwright and a serious eco-architect. In short many are part of the constituency any 'left' project would have to attract. Therefore although ethical consuming, in so far as it is a force for change, must be, as Pepper argues, considered reformist, it is by no means clear that it should be ignored by those on the radical left.

Between Right and Left: Towards a Political Philosophy of Ethical Consumerism

A Significant Phenomenon?

Nevertheless I have located ethical consumers in that contemporarily familiar political position between right and left. It is therefore perhaps appropriate to quote Anthony Giddens[43] concluding that in 'post-scarcity society' '[i]t isn't likely that there will be a general revolt against consumerism ...'

Pepper dismisses eco-consumerism as working '... through a market mechanism ...' and yet it is difficult to imagine that we will not be living in a market economy for the foreseeable future. In such circumstances I see no necessary reason to abandon market mechanisms to the public choice theorists of market liberalism.

Indeed there is reason to believe that morality affects the decisions of a very wide range of those who find themselves in consumer society. Thus Lunt and Livingston[44] say of their research that '[p]eople are continually guided by moral and social issues in their economic choices .... and the relation between everyday economic activity and broader social concerns'; and according to the authors, we have moved from modernism where experts in fragmented specialisms informed society to postmodernism where individuals are responsible. However, and this parallels the theoretical predicament set out above, '... the individual may be given more and more responsibility without the resources or power to act effectively.' This is captured in the authors' summation:[45]

> The people we have talked to during this research are engaged in a debate concerning the nature of identity in consumer culture. The dynamic of debate is a natural milieu for them .... concerning tradition and modernity, freedom and determinism, opportunity and danger. Big issues played out in a domestic setting.

Of course it is possible as Schlegelmilch[46] does to overplay the significance of 'positive' consumer attitudes but it seems to me reasonable to conclude that there is more potential for consumer boycotts and buycotts[47] than has so far been manifest.[48] And because the results of collective consumer action may not always be entirely beneficial there is an added concern. David Meiklejohn,[49] for instance, relates the cautionary tale of consumer concern in the USA about child labour coupled with the possibility of legislation that had 'devastating' consequences in producer countries.

> [G]arment manufacturers [in Bangladesh] reacted to the fear of losing such a major market by sacking an estimated seventy-five percent of all children in the industry. Overnight, children were freed from one kind of child labour but, with few alternatives, they had little option but to seek other, often more dangerous work.

It is for these reasons that the understanding of ethical consumerism is, I would argue, important.

The Rise of the Ethical Consumer?

Whatever name the ethical consumer is given, s/he is invariably characterised as a new phenomenon. Thus David Pepper's[50] 'mushrooming of popularity [of eco-consumerism]' or Bob Worcester's[51] 'rise of the green consumer'. In so far as this implies an awakening of concern, I think it is misleading.

It is well documented that mass political action changes over time. In the post-war period, for instance, it is recognised that a decline in participation in party political activity was accompanied by a significant rise in membership of single issue pressure groups; some activities decline whilst others expand. I take this to be primarily a response to circumstance, although I assume there to be a dialectic process, and therefore not necessarily a fundamental change in ideology.

Since the 1950s, a peak in political involvement, the power of national democratic institutions has waned and along with it people's participation. The deregulation and privatisation of the 1980s, international agreements like the General Agreement on Tariffs and more recently the Multilateral Agreement on Investment are significant contributions to this.[52] These, it is argued, have constrained the traditional collective institutions. As Robert Cox[53] describes this process:

> .... global finance limits the power of governments to carry out policies that might moderate social disparities and maintain the kind of social services that were developed in the richer capitalist countries during the post war decades. [....] The motivation was to encourage a business climate attractive to foreign capital and to match deregulatory moves by other countries in a competitive

175

international financial environment.

The concept of a decline in democratic power at all levels which accompanies globalisation of markets is, of course, a widely disputed theory. It is not my purpose to enter that argument here.

Although ethical consumers may or may not be directly aware of all of these changes or the theoretical debates, some express concerns about the potential of democratic intervention. For example from my case studies, in interview one ethical consumer disapproved of what he saw as the increase in market power and decline in democratic power. He would, he said, join the Green Party if he lived in Germany where they had more influence. Perhaps more significantly another had served as a city councillor in senior positions for many years. He had worked tirelessly for free public transport in the area. At the point where it seemed achievable the entire project was swept away by privatisation in spite of strong public support. He said that he had become disillusioned with the democratic process and resigned.

My point is not, of course, that democratic action should not be pursued. However, many people have experienced what they take as democratic deficit, at the same time the majority of people in Britain as in other affluent countries have experienced, and broadly welcomed, an increase in the scope (commodification), frequency and extent of their consumption (figure 1) through a continual rise in real disposable income. Bertell Ollman[54] more forcefully asserts that '[w]ith the explosive expansion of consumerism - of the amount of time, thought, and emotions spent in buying and selling, and in preparing for (including worrying about) and recovering from these activities - the market has become a dominant, if not *the* dominant, influence in how people act and think throughout the rest of their lives.' Although the term 'consumer' was overworked in the Thatcher years, for most people there is some real sense in which they have increasingly become consumers. From those so inclined, this greater engagement in consumption must surely *invite* political consideration of 'collective' action in the market.

So, at a time when there is a debate about traditional forms of political action being frustrated and many individuals increasingly engage in consumption, have we the circumstances for a small but significant change? I am not suggesting this is a deliberate, considered change of strategy on the part of individuals. This may well be the case with some in say the *New Economics Foundation* but that is not the concern here. I think it is more possibly a lack of incentive or occasionally frustration in one area accompanied by an imperative and experimentation in another. What I particularly want to argue from this is that the 'rise' of the ethical (green or eco-) consumer is more likely to be, or is better understood to be, a continuity of concern with its roots to be found in well established ideologies. To the extent that this notion of a redirection of attention offers a better conceptualisation than portrayals of a 'rise of ...' consumer activism we should be looking for a continuity of ideology.

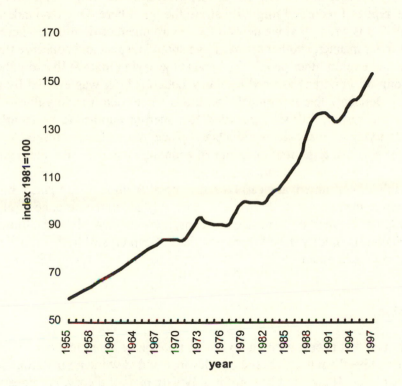

Figure 1   Average consumers' expenditure in Britain 1955-1997 in 'real' terms
Source: Adapted from *Social Trends* 1970, 1981 and 1998, The Stationary Office

Theorising the Roots of Ethical Consumerism

Some heterogeneity is apparent from my case studies such that a coherent ideology of ethical consumerism is not immediately apparent. Among those who responded to my study were lapsed anarchists and a neo-pagan. There was more than one conservative[55] but also generally concerns about loss of tradition were evident. This may be typified by one respondent's belief that 'some things like the local production of small scale special products are good and worth preserving'.

However, when invited to discuss the importance of their ethical consuming, environmentalist and socialist views, including those from the Methodist, Catholic and Jewish traditions, predominated. Some quotations from the replies I recorded might illustrate the point here. One respondent argued that 'it is wrong that we despoil the environment or dominate others' and, in similar manner, another asserted 'we should respect and conserve the earth and not exploit other people'. Likewise the saying that we 'borrow the earth from our children' as used by the Woodcraft Folk was evoked by a further respondent. The notoriously nebulous social democratic values of 'fairness and responsibility' were cited to underpin another respondent's actions. In trying to 'make the world a better place' more than one respondent recited the socialist argument in favour of economic equality, that there are few choices when you are poor.

Ethical consumerism clearly offers a moral critique of capitalism but is reformist in the sense that activists and those engaged in the practice rarely aim to displace the market. In most cases consumers are clear about the limits of their actions to modify the extreme practices of capitalism. In this sense it is not, of course, utopian.

Conclusion

I have argued that if one attempts to link the notion of an ethical consumer with market liberalism it is at best an irrelevance and at worst an irritation or market distortion. It does not fit comfortably with market theory, nor does it contribute towards any revolutionary eco-socialist transformation. We may understand the phenomenon as located politically between Right and Left.

Three points are offered towards a political philosophy of ethical consumerism. Firstly, the 'ethical' in consumerism is not new. Whilst it may be difficult to pin down a precise ideology, many of the roots of ethical consumerism are evident in conservatism, religious and humanist socialism. Secondly, the narratives of ethical consumerism are better understood as socially constructed. They result in and are derived from an interplay of collective and individual action. And finally ethical consumerism is not extricable from the range of politico-economic forms which Ekins sees as constituting New Economics.

My suggestion is therefore that ethical consumerism, in so far as it is a project aimed at change, be located as an extension of collective reformist action within contemporary consumer capitalism. This leaves the 'strategy' open to adverse criticism but within an appropriate political context.

Notes

1   Pepper, David., 'Green Consumerism - Thatcherite environmentalism', *New Ground*, 1989/90.

2   Schlegelmilch, Bido, 'Green, Ethical and Charitable', in Michael Baker (Ed.) *Perspectives on Marketing Management*, 4, (Chichester: John Wiley & Sons, 1994) pp. 57-68.

3   Rob Harrison is co-editor of the *Ethical Consumer* worker cooperative.

4   Gonce, R. A., 'L. E. von Mises on Consumer Sovereignty' in Donald. E. Moggridge (Ed.) *Perspectives on the History of Economic Thought v.3* (Aldershot: Edward Elgar Publishing, 1990) p. 137.

5   Powell, Enoch, *Freedom and Reality* (Kingswood: Elliot Right Way Books, 1969) p. 33.

6   Ekins, Paul, *Sustainable Consumerism, New Consumerism: Theoretical Basis and Practical Application* (London: 1989, New Economics Foundation).

7   Mintel market research produced reports in 1991 and 1994 responding firstly to environmental issues and subsequently also to a broader range of 'ethical' consumer concerns. The second publication is used here: Mintel, *The Green Consumer*, vols. 1 & 2 (London: 1994, Mintel Research).

8   Raphael, D. D., *Adam Smith* (Oxford: Oxford University Press, 1985).

9   Ibid. p. 44.

10   Anderson, Terry and Leal, Donald, *Free Market Environmentalism* (London: Westview, 1991) p. 4.

11   Foxall, Gordon, 'Environment-Impacting Consumer Behaviour' in M. J. Baker (Ed.) *Perspectives in Marketing Management*, 4, (Chichester: Wiley, 1994) pp. 27-53.

12   Brittan, Samuel, 'The green power of market forces', *Financial Times*, May 4th, 1998.

13   Pearce, David, Markandya, Anil and Barbier, Edward, *Blueprint for a Green Economy* (London: Earthscan Publications, 1994).

14   Joseph, Keith and Sumption, Jonathan, *Equality* (London: John Murray, 1979) p. 76. Hayek was, of course, key in reviving the individualist political philosophy. See pp. 10-11 in *The Road to Serfdom* (London: Routledge, 1944). Following this Anderson and Leal note that the right-wing American academic Thomas Sowell advocates that the word 'vision' be used to mean individually held views: Anderson, Terry and Leal, Donald, *Free Market Environmentalism* (London: Westview, 1991). This insistence on individualism is illustrated well by the editor of a series of market liberal tracts published by the Institute of Economic Affairs on environmental issues who assures the reader that no corporate view is being expressed. See, for instance, Bate, Roger and Morris, Julian, *Global Warming: Apocalypse or Hot Air* (London: Institute of Economic Affairs, 1994).

15   Friedman, M and Friedman, R., *Free to Choose* (Harmonsworth: Penguin, 1979) pp. 65-66.

16   Newholm, Terry, 'Low energy light bulbs, markets and ethics', *Philosophy Today* 11, no.28 (1998) pp. 4-5, explores the limited scope for transmitting consumer meaning to producers.

17   Lloyd, Kate, 'Green Consumers: the truth behind the hype', *HPI Research Group* (London: 1992) and current but unpublished work by Deirdre Shaw.

18   Current but unpublished work by Deirdre Shaw at Glasgow Caledonian University shows a majority (>80%) of respondents to a questionnaire are members of an organisation which supports their ethical concerns. Of these respondents the majority are involved with environmental organisations (807) (e.g. FoE; WEN; Greenpeace; Soil Association; HDRA). Other group membership included groups concerned with human rights (357) (e.g. Liberty; Amnesty; Baby Milk Action), religious charities (349) (e.g. Tearfund; Oxfam; Traidcraft; Christian Aid; Save the Children; Third World First), other (e.g. investment) (277), animal welfare (257), "ethical" retailers

(132) (e.g. Out of this World), international development (131) (e.g. WDM), vegetarianism (105) (Vegan and Vegetarian Societies). To be published in *Marketing Intelligence and Planning*.

19   Newholm, Terry, 'Spreading the word', *Green Futures*, Oct-Nov 1997, No.7, p. 17.

20   Pepper, David, 'Green Consumerism - Thatcherite Environmentalism', *New Ground* (1989/90).

21   Pepper, David, *Eco-socialism: from deep ecology to social justice* (London and New York: Routledge, 1993). Table 2.2.

22   Friedman, Milton, *There's No Such Thing as a Free Lunch* (LaSalle, Illinois: Open Court, 1975).

23   Ekins, Paul, *Sustainable Consumerism, New Consumerism: theoretical basis and practical application* (London: 1989, New Economics Foundation).

24   Kurt Baier refers to this strand of thought as supposing humans to be 'psychological egoists' in his contribution, 'Egoism', to Peter Singer (Ed.) *A Companion to Ethics* (Oxford: Blackwell, 1993) pp. 197-204. He shows the emptiness of such a supposition.

25   Etzioni, Amitai, *The Moral Dimension: Toward a New Economics* (London: Free Press, 1988) undertakes a substantial critique of assuming a singular human motivation.

26   Pepper, David, 'Green Consumerism - Thatcherite Environmentalism' , *New Ground* , 1989/90.

27   Friedman, Milton, *There's No Such Thing as a Free Lunch* (LaSalle, Illinois: Open Court, 1975) on p. 17 asserts that because consumers demand products and producers respond, consumers as individuals are responsible for all consequences.

28   Hattersley, Roy, *Choose Freedom: the future of democratic socialism* (London: Penguin, 1987).

29   Joseph, Keith and Sumption, Jonathan, 'Poverty is not unfreedom' in *Equality* (London: John Murray, 1979) pp. 47-52.

181

30   Tawney, R.H., *The Acquisitive Society* (London: Collins, 1961, original 1921).

31   Galbraith, John K., *The Affluent Society* (Harmondsworth: Pelican, 1962) p. 4.

32   Hayek, F.A., *The Road to Serfdom* (London: Routledge, 1944).

33   Pepper, David, *Eco-socialism: from deep ecology to social justice* (London and New York: Routledge, 1993).

34   Gabriel, Yiannis and Lang, Tim, *The Unmanageable Consumer* (London: Sage, 1995), p. 168.

35   I am unable to do justice to David Pepper's critique of eco-consumerism which is set out in *Eco-socialism: from deep ecology to social justice* (London and New York: Routledge, 1993). I agree with much of what he says but believe his polemic approach prevents a full and incisive consideration of the phenomenon.

36   Baudrillard, Jean, 'Consumer Society', in Mark Poster (Ed.) *Selected Writings* (Oxford: Polity Press, 1988). I am thinking here of Baudrillard's critique of Galbraith's concept of human need subverted to excessive consumption by the industrial complex.

37   Heiskanen, Eva and Pantzar, Mika, 'Towards Sustainable Consumption: Two New Perspectives', *Journal of Consumer Policy*, 20, no.4, (1997) pp. 409-442.

38   Schweickart, David, 'Market Socialism: A Defence', in Bertell Ollman (Ed.) *Market Socialism* (New York: Routledge, 1998) uses this argument against utopian socialism, p. 15.

39   Reluctance to develop a consumer theory is almost certainly strongly influenced by Marx's caution against 'proceed[ing] from consumption' where mystification of 'real living conditions' can be ignored. See discussion in Ollman, Bertell, 'Market Mystification in Capitalism and Market Socialist Societies' in Bertell Ollman (Ed.), *Market Socialism* (New York: Routledge, 1998).

40   For instance, Hansen, Ursula and Schrader, Ulf, 'A Modern Model of Consumption for a Sustainable Society', *Journal of Consumer Policy*, 20,

No.4 (1997) pp. 443-469; Ekins, Paul, 'Sustainable Consumerism, New Consumerism: theoretical basis and practical application' (London: 1989, New Economics Foundation); and Harrison, Rob, 'Future Shop', *Ethical Consumer* Nov/Dec 1995: Issue 38, pp. 28-29.

41   See discussion in Gabriel, Yiannis and Lang, Tim, *The Unmanageable Consumer* (London: Sage, 1995).

42   Pepper, David, *Eco-socialism: from deep ecology to social justice* (London and New York: Routledge, 1993).

43   Giddens, Anthony, *Beyond Left and Right* (Cambridge: Polity Press, 1994) p. 248.

44   Lunt, Peter and Livingstone, Sonia, *Mass Consumption and Personal Identity* (Buckingham: OU Press, 1992), p. 166.

45   Ibid. p. 171.

46   Schlegelmilch, Bido, 'Green, Ethical and Charitable' in Michael Baker (Ed.), *Perspectives on Marketing Management*, 4, (Chichester: 1994) pp. 57-68.

47   See discussion in Friedman, Monroe, 'A Positive Approach to Organised Consumer Action: The "Buycott" as an alternative to the Boycott', *Journal of Consumer Policy,* 19, No. 4, 1996, pp. 439-451.

48   Ekins argues that 'the extent to which [progressive consumerism] could transform business practice is hard to overestimate.' Ekins, Paul, 'Towards a progressive market', in Paul Ekins and Manfred Max-Neef (Eds.), *Real-life economics: understanding wealth creation* (London: Routledge, 1992) p. 325.

49   Meiklejohn, David, 'Child Labour', *Ethical Consumer* No.51 (1998), p. 30. For a more positive story of the success of fair trade see Roger Crowe's 'Rich pickings' in *The Guardian* 9 September 1998, G2 pp. 4-5.

50   Pepper, David, 'Green Consumerism - Thatcherite Environmentalism', *New Ground* 1989/90.

51   Worcester, Robert, *International Behaviour and Attitudes to the Environment* (London: 1996, MORI Social Research Institute).

52   See Kevin Watkins' discussion 'Green dream turns turtle' in *The Guardian* 9 September 1998, G2 pp. 4-5.

53   Cox, Robert, 'Democracy in hard times: economic globalisation and the limits to liberal democracy', in Anthony McGrew (Ed.), *The Transformation of Democracy* (Cambridge: Polity Press, 1997), p. 58.

54   Ollman, Bertell, 'Market Mystification in Capitalism and Market Socialist Societies' in Bertell Ollman (Ed.), *Market Socialism* (New York: Routledge, 1998), p. 82 (emphasis in the original).

55   I here take conservatism to be the project set out, for instance, by Ian Gilmour in *Inside Right* (London: Hutchinson, 1997).

Index